What to Do Before You Say "I Do"

Concrete Ideas and Solutions to Create
a Great Start in Your Relationship That
Carries through Your Marriage

Susan Ziggy

authorHOUSE®

AuthorHouse™
1663 Liberty Drive
Bloomington, IN 47403
www.authorhouse.com
Phone: 1-800-839-8640

Published by AuthorHouse 1/28/2013

ISBN: 978-1-4817-0714-5 (sc)
ISBN: 978-1-4817-0713-8 (hc)
ISBN: 978-1-4817-0712-1 (e)

Library of Congress Control Number: 2013900707

This book is dedicated to Eric and Lindsay.
I am very proud of who you became.

I also want to send a special thank-you to my parents, family, and friends who agreed to open up their marriages to share their experiences so others might learn how to succeed in theirs.

Table of Contents

Introduction

I grew up with a father who was a school psychologist. My five other siblings and I were raised to analyze behaviors and discuss why people did what they did. I still analyze why people do what they do and how I can help. This led me to major in education with a minor in psychology in college, where I eventually earned a master's degree in special education from Buffalo State College in New York. I subsequently taught high school special education for fifteen years.

Those years were spent helping my students understand how to get along with others, gain life skills, and modify their behavior (using behavior modification) to learn acceptable ways of getting along with others. I worked with my young adults and loved it until a serious surgery suddenly left me with nerve and muscle damage in my leg. It became increasingly difficult to walk as much as was required for my job. While the spirit was willing, the body gave out, and I had to retire from teaching early.

I searched for jobs that required minimal walking. Before I was a teacher, I'd studied interior decorating, so I returned to that interest and was hired as a designer working for a few guys, providing the ideas for decorating flipped houses. It required minimal walking, and I had a great time deciding color palettes, which walls came down and where architectural details would provide some punch—all without having to do the work. I loved it.

Coincidentally, this new career moved me into a man's world. Obviously, remodeling houses and construction is still a male-dominated field. It was quite eye opening to find out that men really *don't* understand what their wives or girlfriends want. It got me thinking of ways to help them. They would talk to me about their partners, and I always heard the same thing: "Why is my wife mad at me?"; "I don't know what I did wrong"; or even, "Why does my wife hate me?" I would talk to them about the situations they were confronting and suggest a few solutions. They would come back and tell me they tried my ideas and it helped.

More than from all my education and teaching experiences, it was in this world that I learned how the glue that holds marriages together can go brittle and dry up. My experiences as a wife and mother gave me this ability to see through to solutions—as much as my upbringing and my education gave me the thinking process and the language to do so. The life lessons gained from my successes and failures in these relationships were not always easily learned, but even my failures have provided more than I can quantify.

I was married to my first husband for fifteen years and spent five of them in marriage counseling. There I learned more about marriage as a process and divorce as an option. In the end, I realized I wasn't in a good marriage and would not be able to turn it into one. I took what I learned into my next marriage, where I have been very happy, and we are still going strong after fourteen years. My husband has read the book and stated that he learned a few things himself to make our marriage even better. We can still get frustrated with each other from time to time, like any relationship, but that's to be expected. We know it will happen, and so we talk about it and move on.

I wrote this book because my children are at the age where they are thinking about marriage and family. I want to give them the best shot at a healthy relationship by sharing what I have learned throughout my life, education, marriages, and divorce. So I offer these lessons to anyone who is setting out in adulthood with the hope of finding a life partner who will journey with them to the end.

This book will not just tell you to "be kind to your partner," but it will give you clear ideas about what you can do to be kind, especially when it's difficult. I aim to provide specific examples and concrete solutions of why certain personalities work together and some don't, and how to consider alternative pathways in your relationship in order to make it work.

If you are thinking about getting married, a million questions must be swirling through your head and giving you jitters. Questions such as: How can you be sure? Are there ways to know that you have found your life partner? Or are you looking at the *right* life partner? Do your goals and ideals really complement each other? How important are traditions and how do we deal with having different ones? These are good questions to ask, and it is my goal to help you answer them and others that I can guarantee will arise. I hope it will be a useful guide to help you make the best choices for partnership and your marriage happy and successful.

Best wishes on your new adventure ... and *keep this book handy for future reference!*

Chapter 1
It Takes More Than Love

When you ask couples getting engaged or deciding to live together why they are doing that, the answer is always the same. *We love each other.* But what does that mean exactly? This chapter will introduce why it takes more than love to succeed in relationships.

The divorce rate just under 50% would indicate that love alone will not carry you through the difficult times you will face. Nonetheless, according to the US Census Bureau, there were over two million marriages in 2011. More couples, around 18 percent, are also choosing to live together.

So. Why *are* people still getting married? The answer is explained in Maslow's "Hierarchy of Needs." Dr. Abraham Maslow, who studied and wrote on human behavior, said,

Humans need to feel a sense of belonging and acceptance, whether it comes from a large social group or small social connections. They need to love and be loved (sexually or non-sexually) by others. In the absence of these elements, many people become susceptible to loneliness, social anxiety, and clinical depression. This need for belonging is so strong that it can often overcome the physiological (physical) and security needs, depending on the strength of peer pressure.

> This strong need for love and belonging can make you marry out of peer pressure from friends, pressure from parents, or financial security! I say that only to say this: if you understand *why* you choose certain partners but don't fulfill *your* human needs, you are likely to not make the best choices for yourself. I will discuss this further in chapter four.

I attended a few of my children's friends' weddings and was very disturbed by how many were divorced after less than five years. They said they loved each other but couldn't get along. The couples didn't know what to expect from their relationships, what roles they were to play. They thought their love for each other would get them through all the daily routines, discussions, and disagreements commonly found in life.

I started asking why these marriages failed and how I could guide others who had just started a serious relationship or had gotten engaged to avoid the same fate. Some of the marriages, based on the information I received from my children, their friends, and my friends, might have been saved had they learned how to honestly communicate—as well as what to expect—before they walked down the aisle.

If I had known what to expect from my first marriage based on reality and not the fairy tale I was hoping for, I would have made better choices. Remember, I am not a counselor or a psychologist; I am a woman who has been divorced and understands the difficulties involved with all types of relationships, marriage, children, economics, and emotions. I sincerely wish I'd had a book like this before I got married the first time!

Chapter 2
Creating Traditions

I start here because traditions will be discussed in every chapter from here on out. You need to have a clear understanding of these to continue. These routines, rituals, and habits will be referred to as *traditions* because they should be embedded in your relationship just like your cultural traditions are embedded in your family. Cultural traditions include the holidays you celebrate, the occasions on which you do the same thing at the same time, either together or separately. Christmas dinner, Passover Seder, Ramadan fasting, Fourth of July fireworks, Superbowl Sunday—these are just a few cultural traditions that you may or may not observe. Would you break a cultural tradition? Probably not. Do you always feel like participating in these traditions? Probably not. But you do because they are important. Your relationship traditions should not be broken either. That's how important observing traditions are to a successful relationship.

If you start observing these traditions early on in the relationship, it can make the difficult times a bit easier. If you are steadfast, keeping the traditions can even help you avoid conflict about the little things, thus avoiding the big conflicts that usually feed off those little things. These ideas and solutions can make the *work* of your relationship a little easier.

Establishing traditions might even help in other ways, depending on personality type (discussed in Chapter 4). If you and your partner know specifically what to expect from each other, it can be less stressful on you both. For example, if you create a tradition of throwing a party every year and you or your partner is uncomfortable with parties it will get easier because you are both clear on what part you each play, it can be much easier to cope with the stress that comes from throwing a party.

I find couples with the strongest bond are the ones who have created these traditions during the dating through engagement stage of their relationship. Then they have worked at keeping these traditions alive throughout their marriage.

There are two reasons traditions strengthen the marriage. First, they are something you do on a regular basis (like a good habit). Just like brushing your teeth is a good habit that maintains your health, these traditions will become habits that sustain your marriage.

Second, traditions let the partners know what to expect. Just like work, the more you know what's expected, the easier the work (relationship) becomes. If you show up every day at your job and do your work, you are rewarded with vacation time and maybe a raise. Your relationship is no different. You need to show up every day, participate with your partner, and do your work. The rewards will be a long-term relationship. There is fear in the unknown and there is comfort in knowing what to expect!

Here are examples of traditions that should be started from the time you get this book and then followed daily. Some may call these good manners, but not everyone has good manners. These traditions can change that. These are basic practices that should be locked into your relationship because they establish a foundation of love and respect. And they are free, thoughtful, and easy:

- *Always* kiss each other hello and goodbye, at minimum; especially when you don't want to. Feel free to just give kisses intermittently.
- *Always* say please and thank-you! I always thank my husband for dinner when he makes it, and he thanks me. If he forgets, I say, "You're welcome," and then he remembers to say thank-you. You can take bad moments and turn them around immediately *just by saying thank-you!*
- Say "I'm sorry" when you have upset your partner. Taking responsibility in the relationship is *very important* and will make both of you feel much better in the long run. If your partner is upset over something else you can still say "I'm sorry you are upset; can I help?" Your concern will be appreciated, whether you can help or not.
- *Every time* you get up to get a drink or something to eat, ask your partner if they want anything as well!

4

- Use terms of endearment in address, if you are the type to do that: "Can I get you a drink, sweetie?" Be careful with these because it can come out wrong when you get upset. For example, "Yes, *dear!*" Or "Okay, *honey!*" Tone is everything if you don't want your sweet talk to be interpreted as sarcasm.
- Never answer your phones or play with your electronic *toys* when you're out together. You should have each other's full attention. Your partner should be the most important person you want to talk to! The only exceptions are if you have a babysitter or if you are on-call for work!

Sometimes you have to observe these *traditions* when you are upset with your partner. But that's why they are traditions and not just nice things to do. Saying "thank you for getting me a drink," even when you are upset or annoyed with each other, can go a long way in easing tensions and re-establishing respectful communication. These are a must!

Here are a few other examples of traditions you should start early on:

Date Night

Every successful couple I interviewed stated that Date Night was—and still is—important. This is something to look forward to. It's a day or night you set aside for just the two of you. As mentioned earlier, you should not take cell phones, Blackberry devices, iPads, or other *toys*. This is a chance for the two of you to reconnect, catch up on weekly events, *talk*. The only exceptions are: if you have children and your sitter needs to get in touch with you, or your job has you on-call. Anything else should wait until the date is over.

Couples dating or engaged might have the luxury of a weeknight or weekday, but single parents might have only one night to choose from, because of their busy schedules. Whatever you decide, stick to it! Date night becomes even more important as you start to have a family.

Here is something my husband and I did when my children were in their teens. We chose our date night to be Mondays, because the kids were with their dad that night. Every Monday we would struggle over which restaurant to go to. We solved this by picking casual, inexpensive restaurants alphabetically. First week an A restaurant; second week a

B, and so on. This always gave us something to look forward to because it was a night out and we wouldn't have to stress over what restaurant. Sidebar: some of the letters in the alphabet were difficult to find (U was tough), so we just changed the rules so that the particular letter we were stuck on just had to be somewhere in the name of the restaurant.

When we were done with the alphabet, we would start over again and try finding a different A restaurant and so on. We had fun and got to try places we would never have thought to go. It gave us new experiences and lots of memories.

Free Traditions

Here are examples of things to do that only require time. You decide how much time your marriage is worth, compromise, and go from there:

- Go for a drive in the city or country. Whichever area you prefer.
- Take a walk in the park, maybe a neighborhood you want to move into. Hold hands!
- Have a game night with just the two of you. Game night with friends would be another night. If you choose this activity, you could practice the game before the friends' game night. My husband and I did this with Pinochle and reading Trivia Pursuit questions!
- Go hiking.
- Go biking.
- Go sit by a lake, ocean, whatever you have close by.
- If you both enjoy photography, take your camera on your outings and take pictures of each other. It can create fun memories, or at the very least, conversations.
- Read the paper to each other. Each of you can read your favorite parts to each other, then discuss what you have read.
- Read a book together—*this* book is a good one to start with!
- Just sit on your deck, patio, or backyard, just the two of you, and play a game or cards. You could also just talk *alone*.
- Create a weekly dinner menu then go grocery shopping together.
- Be creative and start something you both enjoy. (See who can throw a ball in a cup (beer pong without the beer); have a dance contest.

My aim here is just to offer crazy, ridiculous ideas to let you understand that, in relationships, sometimes you should be ridiculous—it's a great stress reliever.

When I was a single parent with no funds, we would do those activities as a family. We all loved to put on loud dance music and just go crazy. Fifteen years later, my children still talk about our crazy dance contests.

These are great free activities you can do when and if children come along too, but never include them on date night. Family traditions are different from relationship traditions.

Cost-Based Activities

Here are some examples of things to do that do cost money. They can create great memories and open up new lines of communication. You just need to stay open to trying new things. Remember to take turns with these. If your partner picks something from this list, or you make your own list, take turns.

- Take a cooking class together.
- Learn something together—a language, ceramics, pottery, whatever you or your partner want to learn.
- Take turns picking a movie.
- Take dance classes. (Guys, this really is fun! My husband first said no, because he hated dancing. When we started the classes, however, he started to really enjoy it so much that our date night would be going to clubs and practicing our salsa, tango, or whatever dance we learned that week.)
- Take golf lessons together.
- Go to a sporting event together.
- Vacation once a year. If you decide to have children, take them, but remember during that vacation you still have to have your date night!
- Host a large party annually.

My whole family loved this last one. I always hosted Thanksgiving dinner and the New Year's Eve parties. It was great because no one had to worry about where they were going for the holidays or what they were going to do on New Year's Eve. All the women would be in the kitchen bonding over our *traditional* jobs while chatting about what was new in everyone's life. We always had the same jobs and brought the same dishes. One sister would bring different desserts every year just for the fun of it! Another sister always mashed potatoes, and a third would make the salad, and so on. It took a lot of pressure off me, because *I knew what to expect.*

All these traditions can carry over into other areas of your relationship. You will gain more mutual respect, develop a shared sense of humor about the little aggravations, and realize what's important between both of you and with your friends and family.

These traditions are also very helpful if you have a partner who isn't comfortable at large events or parties. I learned this from experience. Once you have the first party, the partner understands their role, knows what to expect, and isn't so anxious or aggravated. After that, they might even look forward to the event, feeling more comfortable—with no fighting involved, because now they enjoy it as much as you.

Money is usually very tight when you are starting out in your relationship. Do whatever your budget allows. At the very least, everyone can afford the free traditions! Date night also goes a long way in showing your commitment to your partner and the relationship. If you have a work conflict on your date night, then stay flexible and have your date on another day or night *that week.* Don't skip it because it didn't fit into your schedule! Make it fit!

The *key* is to create whatever activity or time frame works for you both and then make it a tradition that you can both stick too. If it doesn't become a habit, it is easy for both parties to get lazy and stop working at the relationship. And that can be the start of a lot of problems down the road. Traditions are *that important* in every relationship just like traditions are that important in your culture!

Ask yourself, *What happens if you stop showing up daily for your job?* Things start to fall apart, don't they? Well, it's no different for your relationship. I realize even keeping a date scheduled can be work and everyone seems to be very busy. But I will say this over and over to make sure you understand the importance of this concept: *make the time!* A long-term marriage (relationship) is priceless! Divorce isn't!

Traditions can be established at any stage of a relationship. It's easier to start them early, but, it's also never too late!

Chapter 3
Compatibility Survey

Here are some questions you need to explore before saying "I do."

I based this questionnaire on thirty years of observation, targeted interviews, and personal experience. It is important to answer honestly, and discuss your answers with your partner.

These questions were written to determine how compatible you *might* be. Don't get upset if your answers are not a complete match. You are not supposed to be exactly alike, and the survey was written knowing that you don't *want* all your answers to match. *Just be honest.*

You should take the survey together, because it can help promote discussion. The survey is intended to be an important communication tool as well as a compatibility indicator. Take the survey when you have ample time to discuss your answers together. This is an important tool and not to be rushed through.

Make a quick copy of the survey or shorthand the questions on a piece of paper. For example, honest? Patient? Etc. Write your answers to the survey on a separate piece of paper. When you are done, trade answer sheets and read them aloud to each other. If you hear your answers coming out of each other's mouths, you are more apt to understand each other—and yourself—better. There are no right or wrong answers, thus no test anxiety!

1. Do you consider yourself a patient person? (Do you experience road rage; do you get anxious when you have to wait; how quickly do you get upset over something?)
2. Have you lived on your own prior to your partner? (If yes, for how long?)

3. Do you consider yourself an honest person?

4. Do you consider yourself a good listener?

5. Do you consider yourself highly emotional, moderately so, or reserved emotionally? This can be gauged by how often you cry at movies, or get upset because your partner didn't remember your first date (that's highly emotional!).

6. Are you athletic?

7. How important is it to you that your partner is athletic? Very, somewhat, or not at all?

8. Are you competitive?

9. Do you think a regular date night is important for your relationship (making time in your hectic schedules to spend time with just each other)?

10. If you can't have both (and sometimes you can't), would you rather be right or happy? That is, in an argument, can you back off to avoid a disagreement or do you have to make your point?

11. Do you like to socialize? If so, how often?

12. Do you tend to be more quiet and reserved or rowdy and exuberant?

13. What is your idea of a clean house?
    A. All surfaces cleared and sterilized.
    B. A few papers and magazines on the kitchen counter are fine, but no food mess.
    C. I do the dishes once a day usually, clean the bathroom once in a while.
    D. If I can find what I'm looking for and the house doesn't stink, I'm good.

14. How important is money to you (other than enough to pay your bills). Very, somewhat, not very.

15. Do you have a good sense of humor? Very, sometimes, not often.

16. Do you want children? If so, how many? Under what conditions?

17. Do you think a college education is important for your children? A profession?

18. Are you the life of the party type or quiet and shy?

19. Can you be happy living below your means in order to save for a rainy day (like unemployment, illness, unexpected surprises) or do you expect things to work out for the best?

20. Do you need to take trips every year or do you save until you can afford a special trip?
21. How much credit card debt do you carry? Under $5k, over $5k, over $10k? Be honest with your partner; it's important!
22. Are you generous with money, or do you count every penny?
23. Have you always dreamed of a large wedding or a small and intimate gathering?
24. Are you okay if the woman makes more than the man?
25. Do you come from similar socio-economic backgrounds?
26. Finish this saying: When the going gets tough, I
    A. get going and fight for the goal.
    B. stay cool and work through it.
    C. give up and walk away
27. Are you an optimist or a pessimist? (Do you expect the best outcome in situations or plan for the worst-case scenario?)
28. Do you prefer to text or talk?
29. How affectionate are you? (Not sexually, but in terms of holding hands, kissing, touching)?
    A. In public:
        i. Very
        ii. Sometimes
        iii. Not often
        iv. rarely
    B. In private:
        i. Very
        ii. Sometimes
        iii. Not often
        iv. Rarely

When you are done with this survey, hand your answers to your partner and read what each other wrote out loud. This is a great time to discuss the similarities and the differences in your answers. What do you think about your partner's answers? How did it feel to hear your own read by the person you love? How did you feel reading your partner's answers? Be sure to discuss each answer. Discuss why you both feel the ways that you do ... without judgment!

Let this survey and the discussion the two of you have about your hopes and dreams, preferences and limitations guide you. What can you accept in yourself and each other? What can you change about yourself? Be sure to acknowledge and have fun with the areas where your similarities lie.

Consider saving your questions and answers. It will be fun and interesting to go back to this survey in five years to see how much you have grown and what issues have blossomed. Take another look every fifth anniversary after that.

Chapter 4
Compatibility

Of course you and your partner feel or think you are compatible; that's why you are thinking marriage. What makes you compatible? Do you share similar goals? Go back to the survey to remind yourself what questions you felt made you and your partner compatible. Compatibility goes beyond your feelings for each other, and is greatly dependent on your individual personality traits.

In this chapter, I discuss what personality traits may or may not be compatible. This is the time where you want to be completely honest about who you are and *not who you think your partner is looking for*. With some things, opposites attract, because opposing traits can bring balance to a relationship. Again, be honest; maybe who you *truly* are is more compatible than who you think your partner wants you to be.

Take a moment to give yourself a quick test! Ask your partner what makes the two of you compatible. A man's answer may be simple: "You are nice, and we get along." Clear and concise! A woman's response might contain more feeling adjectives. She may respond with words like "you are kind, attentive, funny, hard-working," and so on. If you pay attention to your partner's answers, you will get big clues into the way they think!

As you get to know each other better and as the years go by, the ways you get along or don't get along will start to show. The way you handle these differences can make your relationship better, using the right tools! So I suggest you recognize these similarities and differences right from the start, rather than holding out to change your partner once you've nabbed them.

What are the tests for compatibility? In my opinion, it boils down to a handful of categories: extroversion/introversion; optimism/pessimism;

A-type/B-type; and values. You can determine, with these personality traits, how compatible you may be. Remember, almost every personality trait has a low-, medium-, and high-range of that particular trait. Think about where you and your partner fit and do you complement each other?

Extroverts & Introverts

Extrovert is the first personality type. They are comfortable meeting new people and comfortable in new situations. They make friends easily, will talk to strangers waiting in line or on the street. They are considered outgoing or "the life of the party." People generally enjoy being around them for that reason.

There are ranges in this personality type, of course, and you might find yourself somewhere along a continuum. Someone who enjoys social events, for example, and is friendly and active but does not have to be the center of attention is an extrovert at a low level.

Another person might enjoy parties and socializing and go so far as to add a spark to those parties in a way that doesn't exclude others. This person could be a medium extrovert.

The extrovert who goes to every social event and needs to be recognized the minute they arrive by making a grand entrance is a high-level extrovert.

And then there is the person who is loud and obnoxious, usually drunk, and doesn't let anyone get a word in edgewise. There could be many reasons for this behavior, but for simplicity's sake, let's just call them an extreme extrovert. They would have a hard time developing a good relationship with anyone but themselves.

Introverts are the opposite. They tend to stay within their circle of friends, are comfortable staying home, shy and quiet at parties, and don't feel all that comfortable meeting new people. This type of personality can be comforting to an extrovert, because they can provide a calming influence for their partner. The extrovert can also help the introvert feel more comfortable by including them in conversations with new people.

There are also ranges in this personality type, obviously. A low-level introvert may not be comfortable attending parties on their own, but if their partner encourages them, they will attend, staying close to their partner initially. After they assess the situation and become more comfortable they will walk around and talk to their good friends without the partner.

A medium-range introvert may or may not want to attend social gatherings unless they know almost everyone who is attending. They are very quiet at parties and most people may not know they are there. They can bring a certain serenity to the conversation and are capable of making people around them feel calm, if they are familiar with you.

The high-level introverts are people who are not comfortable meeting strangers, with or without their partner. The will stay in one location and people would have to come to them. They are only comfortable within their own environment and don't feel the need to meet new people. They may have to be coaxed into trying new things as well.

These two personality types can be a great match and bring balance to a relationship. You will need to pay attention to the level of your personality traits, however; you will both feel unsatisfied ultimately if either of you feel hemmed in or bulldozed by the other's comfort zone.

A low to mid-range extrovert and a low to mid-range introvert can forge a complementary relationship, because each can bring out the best in the other. The extrovert can bring the introvert into conversations and make their partner feel more comfortable participating in groups. On the other hand, the introvert can help set limits on the number and type of social events the couple attends.

Be leery however, two extremes in these personality types can create conflict and disaster.

If you pair an extreme *extrovert* with an extreme *extrovert*, initially they may enjoy their similarities, but it will get old and exhausting down the road. You can only attend so many parties before the same stories you tell get boring. As people mature at different rates, one may change their enthusiasm for the party life while the other might not.

The same would apply to two high-level introverts. They may enjoy the quiet life and staying home, but that could become boring after a while as well. There would be no opposite force to encourage socialization and exploration of new events. As long as they are both aware of this and truly don't think it will become boring, it can work, but more than likely would not be a healthy relationship. Without growth through learning new things, life is boring.

The high-level extrovert and a high- to mid-level introvert more than likely wouldn't work. This pairing would probably never happen. If they were introduced by a mutual friend, they probably wouldn't connect because the extrovert would want to converse and the introvert wouldn't. This pair would only frustrate each other. The high-or even mid-level introvert may become the target of embarrassment by the high level extrovert, who can feel hemmed in and embarrassed by the more reserved partner and might start exploiting the introvert's weaknesses at social events—especially if the extrovert becomes intoxicated. A high-level introvert can be an easy target for this type of extrovert if they succumb to a tendency toward bullying behavior. They can be rude and insulting to their partner as part of their entertainment. This can transfer over into daily situations, and respect becomes intermittent, if not obsolete. You don't ever want to make your partner feel uncomfortable, if you truly respect them. *Everything in moderation* should be the mantra here.

If you are both high-level extroverts, you could have issues at social events, especially if you find yourselves fighting for the spotlight. If you both want to be the center of attention and you try to out-do each other, it can become very competitive, frustrating, and embarrassing for your partner and your friends. This is not respecting your partner!

This should be considered a *red flag* when it comes to a long-term relationship—particularly if drinking is involved. Have you ever seen an extroverted couple when they were both intoxicated? How did that make you feel? Give yourself plenty of opportunities and various scenarios to determine if you can maintain respect for each other.

Two medium-level extroverts, on the other hand, can make a great match. You both enjoy social events and are comfortable meeting new people. You enjoy the excitement of trying and doing new things. If you can both *share* the spotlight as partners and not competitors, you can have a lot of fun together and with others, particularly if you avoid a tendency to be competitive. No matter what type you are, you need to respect each other's uniqueness and allow the other to shine—better yet, to enjoy each other's shining.

Two low-level extroverts can also make great match. They enjoy going out together, trying new things, and are good at socializing. They feel comfortable at parties, but don't need to be the life of the party. They are very similar to the low-level introvert. The extrovert would however, feel more comfortable socializing with folks they have met only once, while the low-level introvert would feel more comfortable interacting with people they have met several times.

Two introverts can also be a good match. Although they certainly wouldn't force each other to get out and socialize, they are comfortable being with just each other, a few friends, and family. They tend to be laid back and don't get excited often, or at least don't show a high-range of excitement. In my opinion, two introverts at the low and medium levels would be a good match. These types are on an even keel in their relationship and are comfortable not having the stimulation of outside influences. In fact, while extroverts seem to need the stimulation of others to feel vital, social activity can feel over-stimulating to introverts and require too much recovery time to fit into a tight schedule.

The main thing to keep in mind is that you need to accept and respect your partner's ways to being in the world. No one is right or wrong, so be sure to ask yourself honestly how much you can enjoy the differences between you in the long term.

***

Another point to remember is that everyone's personality has other characteristics that influence who they are. These traits and tendencies can mitigate or enhance each other.

Optimists & Pessimists

Most of you have heard the expression "Is your glass half full or half empty?" That is the simple definition of an optimist and a pessimist.

In psychological terms, optimists feel they can overcome tough situations and also appreciate their victories more. When an optimist has a victory, they carry it into other aspects of life, bringing more confidence to other situations.

In contrast, pessimists seem to believe that the one victory was just that, an isolated victory, an unusual success. They have difficulty transferring it to other aspects of their lives. They doubt their abilities to overcome tough situations, and it can undermine everything they do. They tend to see the worst in every situation. They also tend to have more anxiety in their life.

Remember there are ranges to each of these personality types as well.

First, I will explain the levels of an optimist. I am an example of an high level optimist. When I became disabled, people couldn't believe how I took it in stride—after I finished the grieving process (which took two years)—and made the best out of a horrible situation. It still baffles friends and family how optimistic I can be while living in pain. I never stop trying new things, because I believe I can work through anything. *If life gives you lemons, build a lemonade stand.*

An high level optimist (from a pessimistic point of view) can be annoying to live with, because they always have to find the best in every scenario. I have been told that I can be naïve or unrealistic because not everything can have a bright side. I agree with that only when it comes to terminal cases like cancer. I still try to find the proverbial *light in that tunnel.*

The normal-range optimist sees things as possibilities and also makes the best out of situations. They don't tend to get upset easily because they try to find the best solution in almost every situation. They have a positive outlook on life and try to work through everything. *They would make lemonade out of lemons.*

A low-range optimist might see the bright side in one category of things but the down side in others. One of my sisters would be a good example. She sees the good in situations that affect her—just don't get her started on government issues. There she is a classic pessimist. *When life gave her a lemon, she sold it, and made some money.*

A low-level pessimist is someone who sits on the border of the glass half full. They worry about new situations. They may ask themselves: How will I do? Will it be too hard for me? They see the bad first and, after several repetitions, can lessen their trepidation and see some good. They can also sway between an optimistic and pessimistic point of view in some situations. They can appreciate a good moment in a play or sporting event, but then see the whole event as negative. Their joy can be short-lived.

The mid-range pessimist struggles to find the good in situations. They worry about almost everything they do and will, more than likely, be negative about it. They struggle to see how situations can end well. They expect them to end badly.

High-level pessimists wear their hat so low they wouldn't be able see much sunshine even on a sunny day. The glass is not only half-empty, but no water at all is on the way! They don't tend to express joy; everything is doom and gloom. They tend to look at the negative side of life even when proven otherwise. *The Eeyore type,* if you've ever read *Winnie the Pooh,* may have difficulty establishing close relationships because they are so negative.

Two optimists at any level would be a good match, in my opinion. They can both see joy in many situations and laugh at other situations. They are happy-go-lucky type people.

An optimist and a low-level pessimist may also be a good match. They bring different views to different situations and conversations. When I was in counseling, one of the counselors thought my first husband (mid-range pessimist) and I (high level optimist) could be a good match. He felt that it could bring balance to the relationship.

Unfortunately that wasn't our only issue, which brings up an important condition in compatibility. Being compatible in one area does not always mean you are compatible over all—no matter how optimistic you are. A lifelong relationship cannot be based on only one area of who you are or how you are compatible. It must be built on several.

Two extreme pessimists may not be a good match, because neither one may be able to see the bright side when you hit a snag, and that doesn't bring balance to the relationship, but rather makes it too easy to walk away. If you are both people who worry about situations, when would the worrying end?

On the other hand, moderate pessimists might feel comfortable together because they view life the same way. Be aware of this combination because you will probably lead an uneventful life. You may stay home more than if you were with an optimist. If you are both agreeable to that and the other compatibilities align it could be a good match.

Again, remember that this is only one of the compatibilities; you should have several that are good matches to make an overall match.

Type-A & Type-B Personalities

If you are a *type-A* personality, you are comfortable getting involved in something or doing something continually. You are likely competitive. You feel the need to do it all! You might not even be comfortable sitting down and watching a movie all the way through, because you have too many other things to do. You are comfortable with chaos, and calmness can make you uneasy.

If you fit this definition, ask yourself why you think you have to always be busy. Do you have a strong need to be in charge? Do you feel you are the only one who can *"get it done"*? Do you have trouble taking direction from others? If you answered yes, you are probably a type-A personality. Type A's, by definition, appear to have large egos when the opposite is true. They have fragile egos and feel the need to work harder in order to gain approval, usually from approval lacking in childhood.

Most of us know people who are driven to succeed in everything they do. If you look deeper you will usually find that person can be a bully due to insecurity in unresolved issues from childhood. It almost always stems from a strong need for approval from childhood that is now transferred into adulthood.

Type-B people have more relaxed personalities and tend to be friendly with cohorts. They are comfortable doing a good job at work and may or may not need to put in extra hours. It would depend on the job. My son and daughter are both type-B personalities. They are both in sales, and that usually does require extra hours; however, they don't bring their work home. Home is their relax time.

Type-Bs usually have healthier egos and prefer peace over chaos. They understand that they don't need to be right or busy all the time. They are more flexible to changes in situations and don't get stressed as often as a type A. They are also considered easy-going and capable of compromise.

Here is another example of where opposites can attract. A *type-B personality with a type-A* could be a good match depending on other variables. Type-B is less competitive and may be able to help their partner slow down, enjoy movies, vacations, or anything else. The type-B can also be a strong source of support for the type-A partner's need to achieve. The *power behind the throne,* as it were.

Whether male or female, a B-type can appreciate the take-charge attitude of the A. Some type-Bs may also find comfort in not having to make decisions; therefore it may not be an issue. Sidebar: As you will see in my interviews in the appendix, pay attention to the type personalities that have made it and who was the type-A and who was the type-B in the relationship. Similarly, the A personality can appreciate the B's ability to slow life down a little and alleviate some of that type-A stress.

Difficulties can arise in the match, however, if the type-A partner does not respect the type-B partner. Here is where the challenge lies. It would depend, again, on what other qualities they both possess. The type-A will, more than likely, want to take control of the relationship. The B-type has to find a way to hold their own without challenging that control directly. Can the type-A compromise? Keep these challenges in mind: depending which type you are, if you are able to respect the less-achievement-oriented partner as your equal, or if you are good at handling a strong person with a sensitive ego, then it could be a very good match. You will be able to work well together and balance the relationship by bringing out the best qualities in each personality.

Two *type-A personalities* may or may not be a good match. It would depend on your other compatibility traits. Can you compromise? Are you both respectful of each other's accomplishments? Are you both highly competitive? When will you make time for each other? Do you both need to be in charge? Are the two of you too busy with work and outside interests to spend a lot of quality time together? Would that be an acceptable arrangement? If you both respect each other and your respective work ethics, it might be fine. If you don't feel the need to spend *quantity* time together, expect you won't and accept that, it might not present a big problem. Both of you will have the freedom to follow your own pursuits and still come home to an understanding partner.

Type-A personalities' conflicts may be fighting for control of the relationship. They are more comfortable knowing what everyone around them is doing and like to keep schedules. This can cause problems if you both want control. Remember this type likes to be challenged. Knowing all these things about yourself and your partner will help in determining your compatibility. Respect for each other and compromising may become an issue, so pay attention to that quality early in the relationship!

Two *type B's* can also be a great match. They would take similar approaches in work and play. They would have ample time to spend together if they chose to (remember, you will want space too), and they are both able to compromise, which is important. They tend to be happy people, so when conflict does arise (and it will) they would both rather be happy than right. This can lead to a quicker resolution in tense situations.

Values

- **Mutual respect.** The habit of showing respect needs to start the first day! Every couple I interviewed that has been married more than twenty years told me, without exception, that mutual respect is a *must* have. I couldn't agree more!

How do you know if your partner *respects* you? You know you have respect from your partner if they listen to your opinions and don't judge what you have to say. Judging would be saying something like "That's a stupid idea; why would you ever think that?" (while rolling their eyes); "Do you even know what you are talking about?" And so on.

For example, my first husband and I were discussing our religious and political views and opinions on abortion with our friends. He told me my opinions were stupid. He wouldn't even listen while I defended my views, so I just stopped talking. When my girlfriend said the same thing two minutes later, he agreed with her. That was a huge lack of respect!

If this sounds familiar, you will need to work on that *before* you get married. How you and your partner handle your differences early on can go a long way in creating a healthy and long-lasting relationship. If it *can't be worked out*, walking out may be a best solution!

- **A sense of humor.** When talking to people over the years about relationships, they all wanted a partner with a good sense of humor. A good sense of humor can help defuse tension and conflict. It is therapeutic for your health and your relationship.

Everyone I have ever asked has said that either their or their partner's sense of humor got them through difficult times. I know I used my sense of humor to get me out of tense situations with my students. It also gets me out of tense situations in my relationships.

Humor means different things to different people, however. You might consider some humor inappropriate or not funny while others are finding it very funny. Think about your favorite comedian; maybe it's Andrew Dice Clay, who's known for his crude humor about women, saying things some men might think but most dare not say; or Robin Williams, the hyperactive funny man who wears you down with his rapid-fire imagination; or Ellen DeGeneres, who's down-to-earth self-deprecating humor might get you laughing at your own foibles. Can you see what I'm getting at? You need to determine what "sense of humor" means to you. A *compatible* sense of humor is great in any relationship.

Sarcasm, defined as *mean humor,* is funny to some, while others think it is just mean! It can be funny to any of us at some time or another, particularly when it is self-deprecating. It is not so funny when it's aimed at you. The best comedians who use sarcasm aim the jokes at themselves. If you enjoy sarcastic humor in your relationship, make sure it's aimed at yourself and not your partner. It can work against you in the long term. *Hurting each other for fun is a bad habit to get into.*

My first husband and I used sarcastic humor. His was aimed at me and mine aimed at him. We laughed while our marriage was good, but, once we started having problems, it wasn't funny, but mean and hurtful! I came to understand how destructive sarcasm was and changed my humorous ways!

It's very helpful in a relationship if at least one of you has a good sense of humor or if you both find the same things funny. If my husband and I are having a useless argument or debate, I will say or do something silly. He turns his focus on me, forgets the conversation, and all is good again. If you can both actually laugh at yourselves in the moment or the tough situation you might be in, at any given time, that's the best kind of sense of humor to have.

- **Live in the *now* and not the past.** I have heard this from counselors and experienced it with my personal relationships. People and situations change, whether it's your competitive nature, ideas you once held, or the belief systems you had when you met. Things or ideas you once believed in may not be what you believe in now. Were you the same person in high school? Probably not.

Avoid saying things like, "When we first met, you hated getting flowers, jewelry, going to movies, etc., so I'm not going to start getting them now." If your partner asks for flowers or wants to go to a movie, do it without bringing up what they said in the past! What they want today can change tomorrow. I know, because I fit into that category!

By the same token, an old argument should stay that way. In the past. Don't bring up the list of old hurts every time a new one arises. Accept who each other is *now*. If the change brings up a sore topic, then use humor and say something cute (you're so funny, you did it again) to let them know you notice that they changed their mind again. Make sure you use a humorous tone! And ladies, this is why it's so important for you to be clear and concise about what you want and how you feel. If things have changed, make it clear.

Your new mantra could be, "What happened or was said yesterday is done and over, today is all we can change, and we don't know what will happen tomorrow." If you said something hurtful yesterday or argued about something, settle it that day! Start fresh today and change how you can handle it better for tomorrow!

- **Socioeconomic status** (class), **culture** (ethnicity, nationality), **creed** (religion, philosophy), **and regional issues need acknowledging.** Do you share the same or similar backgrounds in your upbringing? How and where you were raised can be an area for conflict, but it doesn't have to be if you realize one is not *normal* and the other *wrong*. If you have preferences or changes you hope to make, get it out in the open or look for someone who shares them already. For example, I'm a stickler for good grammar and good manners. It was important to me to find someone who was compatible. And I did!

Do you both enjoy similar interests, likes and dislikes? If you can stay flexible because of their other great qualities, you may learn to appreciate their interests—maybe not like it, but appreciate it. I used to hate hockey. I thought it was a rough and violent sport. But the man I love is a hockey official, and needless to say, he loves hockey. I would watch the games with him, and he taught me about the game. The more I started to understand the game, the more I liked it. I learned to love hockey!

Are your political or religious beliefs compatible? These overall perspectives may not be important to you at all, but for some relationships, it can be a deal breaker if one partner is steeped in a cultural custom that the other isn't comfortable with. Or is not steeped in one the other requires. You may feel not sharing a worldview is okay now, but think long-term. Stay flexible and willing to compromise should it come down to that.

- **Do you share the same work ethic?** Is one of you high energy, and the other low energy? Is one of you a couch potato, while the other is working? Is one partner working on the house while the other is playing? This can become irritating to the partner who is working on things that should be shared.

With women and men sharing the breadwinning nowadays, more and more couples are establishing household responsibilities from the get-go. If one partner finishes their work early, are you okay with them sitting and watching TV the rest of the day? Are you both willing to help when the rooms need to be painted? Furniture moved? Spring cleaning done?

All these issues should be determined before you make a large commitment to each other. And, most important, stay *flexible* with each other, discussing options and choices openly when a situation arises works towards resolutions.

Chapter 5
The 7 Stages in a Relationship

There are stages you will go through. You go from dating to engaged, married, and so on. If you are in the dating or engagement period, then you got this book at the perfect time.

This chapter will discuss what you can expect at various stages in your relationship. Remember, the more you know about what to expect, good or bad, the better off you will be. It is helpful to remember, each stage has its own *work*. Just like in a job, you will need to know what the work is, what tasks are involved, what's expected of you in the relationship. Also just like in a job, the work gets easier as you show up daily, gain more experience and become better at it.

It is very important that both men and women read this book. Out of the hundreds of men I have interviewed, only one has ever read a single self-help book. Guys, make this your first! Whether the two of you choose to read this book together or separately, reading it will let your partner understand the level of your commitment, and you will know what they are talking about when your partner brings up points from this book! Communication is very important at every step of a relationship.

Stage I: Dating (The Honeymoon Period)

You have just started dating or have been dating for a few months. You can't wait to see each other. You start thinking this could be *"The One."* At this stage, presumably, you love to kiss, hold hands, have loads of laughs and hot sex. You enjoy long conversations or just sitting together watching TV or going out together. This is called the "honeymoon period" in a relationship. You tend to put your best foot forward and let little annoyances slide. Here is where your foundation for your potential future starts. It is very important to be honest with your partner. Don't let the little stuff slide. If it bothers you, tell them in a thoughtful but honest way.

Be careful also not to set the gift-giving bar too high in trying to impress your potential partner, ladies and gentlemen. This is really another honesty issue. If you can't afford an expensive gift, choose to *do* something thoughtful instead. Your partner might be more impressed by a thoughtful partner more than the gift itself. A thoughtful gesture will tell them who you are, not what you have! Making your partner dinner, giving a massage or foot rub, these would be examples of thoughtfulness. If you want to score big, when your partner says they love something while you are shopping together, write it down and buy it for their birthday or anniversary. The hard part is remembering where you wrote it down!

If you choose to start out with expensive gifts, they might become expected down the road. People tend to feel they have to out-do their previous gifts (damn commercialism!) and that can lead to financial problems or unrealistic expectations if your finances change.

Remember to start small ... but thoughtful. A strong relationship cannot be built by blowing your intended's mind with overwhelming gift-giving. Show them you are thinking of them with affection, respect, and hopes for more connection in the future. If you throw the store at them, it puts you both under too much financial weight.

In this stage, you also run the risk of convincing yourself that their annoying habits are cute, or at the very least, tolerable. Again, be honest ... with yourself. If you feel your dating partner is overly sensitive or too emotional, let them know (examples are helpful) and talk about it. If you feel your partner is already trying to change you, and you barely know each other, let them know that doesn't feel good and talk about it ... or *walk away*. If you don't want to watch sports all day let them know. If do-it-yourself home projects don't sound like good weekend activities to you, let them know. You need to discuss compromises (chapter 8).

The honeymoon period may last a month or six months, but rest assured, it will end, and reality will set in. If you expect it and know it's coming then you know your relationship is "normal" and won't stress or worry when the relationships shifts gears.

Stage 2: When reality starts

If you progress beyond the honeymoon period, then this is when the relationship work gets more serious. This may be the point that you realize your partner is worth getting to know on a deeper, more realistic level. You may start to argue at this stage, but you will either feel confident that you can resolve these conflicts or that your partner will change once you are married. Beware of building your future on fantasies. People do not change their unwanted behaviors after they get married. In fact, sometimes they can intensify, because they feel a sense of security by being married. They may feel they don't have to change—after all, you accepted them the way they were. That is why honesty from the beginning is so important. If you are *not* honest about recognizing flaws in yourself or your partner *from the beginning,* it will lead to larger problems in the long term.

Some people feel the need to do everything at this stage to show their potential life partner how they can "do it all." I have witnessed young women in new relationships wanting to impress their partners by cooking, cleaning, purchasing gifts for birthdays, taking care of planning all the events, holidays, everything. I have seen young men cooking, cleaning, running errands, *shopping* with their partner, and negotiating deals to impress their potential mates that they are a good catch. Ladies and gentlemen, you need to *stop doing that, unless that is honestly who you are!*

Everyone wants to feel both useful *and* desired, so let each other know you *want* to help, on the one hand, and what you need help for. If you are honest from the beginning it will benefit the relationship and can make life easier and/or more fun.

This is where it's helpful too, if you have each lived on your own before the relationship starts. You both already know how much work is involved in taking care of a house or apartment, doing laundry, grocery shopping, and maybe making meals. This can lead to more respect for your partner. If one (while the partner worked) spent the day cleaning, making food, and did the laundry, the other partner knows how much effort and work was involved. It will be appreciated more if you have lived on your own. Some men who have lived on their own prior to a relationship have learned to cook meals and find they really enjoy it. This can be an asset in a relationship!

This early stage is a crucial stage in a relationship, because it sets the footprint for the type of future you will have. The earlier you establish traditions, guidelines, rules, and expectations for what each of you want—*and don't want*—the better. If you plan a party, do you wait until an hour before the party to invite your friends? Hopefully not; you would invite them when you *started* planning the party. Your relationship is no different. The earlier you start, the better you will be prepared as the relationship progresses.

Stay flexible to changes and be honest about your feelings. As you read further, you will get more suggestions and ideas on how to do this.

Stage 3: The Engagement Period

This is the commitment stage. These first three stages are also the best time to start the traditions. You now feel you are compatible and can go through the next fifty or sixty years with your partner. That's a mighty long time so it's important here to make an *eyes-wide-open* decision.

This is where you start establishing the *type* of marriage you will have. You will definitely want to look more closely at the red flags or warning signs (chapter 10) that tell you some of the behaviors you have been tolerating should be rethought. There might be something you really *can't* live with long term. Are you marrying your partner for the right reasons? Remember Maslow's Hierarchy of Needs?

If you have been tolerating your partner's flaws because you feel they are *The One,* then if you haven't been honest, it's time to get real about your feelings. At this stage, if you continue to placate your partner, you are lying to them about who *you* really are. That is very unfair. You need to be who you are and not who you think your partner wants you to be!

Hopefully, at this point you have become more honest about those annoying habits that once seemed so cute. You have had your first arguments and have begun to learn a particular way of settling them. So, do you feel they were settled fairly? Did you feel heard? Did you feel safe, confident, okay with telling your partner how you felt? Did you feel it was open communication? Did you feel able to listen as well? Were you spoken to in a way that you could hear what they were saying? Did you feel respected for your views?

These are all things you should be looking for in a long-term partner.

This is the time you are learning more about who your partner is. You should not assume you already know everything about each other, but should be paying close attention to important issues like compromising, arguing fairly, and trusting your partner. Are you *both* willing to do what it takes at this stage?

Some people however, move to stage 3 because they feel it's time— they are getting older, and feel it is the only way to hang on to their partner. If you honestly feel that way, then you need to rethink *why* you feel that way and talk about it with your partner. Is peer pressure taking over? Are all your friends getting married and starting families, so you feel you need to as well?

You need to communicate your feelings and fears to your partner. Most people experience these same fears, so you are not alone. Your partner may share your fears but is afraid to tell you! Trust that your partner loves and respects you, then you can both figure out (with a plan) how to get through the issue and help you through this without judgments. If they can't and become defensive, then maybe you should listen to what they are *not* saying (body language, eye contact) and start your conversation over.

Do you have such a strong need to belong to someone that you forget your own needs? Were you independent, had a lot of friends, a happy person? If so, your friends or family might be able to help you answer the questions you have about compatibility and suitability more than your partner. It's the "can't see the forest through the trees" syndrome. Your emotions and excitement are high at this stage, so you don't tend to think logically. Your family or friends may be able to *see the forest through the trees*.

That's another mistake I made in my first marriage. I wanted to find someone to take care of me. He had a good job and was fun to be around, and that's all I thought I needed. I didn't pay attention to the red flags, despite my older sister telling me he wasn't the right guy for me.

Some couples also feel the need to marry for financial reasons or a place to live. If you marry your partner for financial security, that can shift the balance of a partnership. It won't be based on equality. Your partner can become more demanding of your time or even disrespectful, because they might believe the person with the money can wield the power. You don't want that. Partnership should be equal ownership of the relationship.

Sometimes people feel pressured to marry by their partner, parents, or friends. Both partners can be guilty of this. It's not always the women delivering the pressure anymore. My daughter was faced with this dilemma. Her boyfriend of eight years felt it was time to get married and start a family. My daughter however was starting a successful career and wasn't ready. They eventually broke up. I give her credit for realizing she wasn't ready, even if her long-term boyfriend was. Women may feel pressured by their biological clocks Try hard not to succumb to that pressure before you are *honestly* ready. For whatever reason, if one partner is not ready, but peer, parent, or other pressure tells them they need to marry anyway, it could end badly.

Whoever is pushing for a long-term relationship with a partner who isn't ready, needs to discuss options and solutions. There's that communication issue again! Marriage is for life, if you have to wait until you are forty to find that special person, then wait.

This is the stage where you need to sit down and work out these issues. Set a plan (see chapter 8) to clarify how well things are working and how to maintain what works or improve what doesn't with your traditions. Revise an existing plan at this stage if you can identify things that aren't working. This is where you and your partner need to stay flexible and work out the kinks in your plan. You don't think I got this book right the first time, do you? I had to revise and rewrite a few times to make it as clear as I could. Your relationship is no different. Revise what's not working in your plan and keep what is. Consult with a professional when you hit snags in the plan and can't figure out a solution that makes you both happy. Couples counseling can make a huge difference at the beginning ... *before* the hurts build up beyond repair.

Many of the men I have spoken to, admit this can be the time they are trying to avoid the issues. They may tell you they don't have any, they just want things to stay the same. That will never happen, because situations change, people mature. Were you the same person you were in high school? Probably not; things change! Both partners need to participate in devising the plan.

Remember, the more work you do now at the beginning of your relationship (like it's your job), the easier it will be later, because you are starting to establish patterns of behavior and traditions. You will also have a clearer idea of what you expect at this stage and how to handle it. This is where the book can guide you into an eyes-wide-open dialog about what you both expect for the future. At this stage, hopefully, you can tell your partner how you feel and you both will still feel loved, secure, and respected.

Stage 4: Marriage

Usually considered the longest and most difficult stage to get through (this would be a whole other book), the wedding and chaos are over. You are settling into a lifelong commitment with the person you have chosen to go through life with. Eventually, the sex can become less frequent (sorry, it's true) and routines established.

Expectations can also change during this stage if you allow them to. You may stop kissing each other goodbye or hello every time. You know the old joke, now that I'm married I can get fat! That is not true! Do you care if your partner stops kissing you every time one of you leaves or if you stop saying and hearing "thank you or I'm sorry"?

Remember, like your job, you need to show up every day and put the work in so you get paid. You are expected to arrive at your place of business ready to work. Your relationship is no different. Be there for your partner (show up), pay attention to what's going on in the relationship (put the work in), and it will yield a healthy and happy relationship (payday!). Don't start becoming complacent. The plan was established—you both understand what's expected—and your traditions have been in place for a while. Make the effort every day to arrive at your marriage with kindness.

Stage 5: Married with Children

If you decide to have children (an intention you should have discussed when you took the survey), your relationship expectations will need to be revised—but not abandoned. You may become so engrossed in the love you have for your children, you forget each other. *Never do that.*

The risk here is you start neglecting relationship needs, the connection you shared just the two of you. You might stop maintaining traditions, because the baby takes all your time and energy. If this happens, your marriage *will* suffer. How much more energy does it require to still be thoughtful and get your partner something to drink when you get up to get yourself something? If you don't continue the traditions you started and show your love for one another, treating each other with affection, respect, and the commitment to connect, *trust me*, your children will suffer too. This I know from personal experience. Children learn only three ways: by example, by example, and by example! You are their example.

Your children, believe it or not, will likely only want to spend time with you until they get to middle school or high school. At that point, you usually become a hotel, bank, and if you're lucky, a consultant. If you have been neglecting your partner for those fifteen years because you have been too busy raising your children, you may find yourselves in trouble. Make sure your *life* partner is always number one! This is also being a good role model for your children. They learn that their partner (when they are adults) should always be respected and enjoyed by the example you showed them.

A counselor once told me the best way to teach your children about relationships was to show love and respect for you partner. That was profound for me at the time, and I remember that from twenty years ago. I have also experienced the truth in that statement.

Relationships will always have their ups and downs. If you are prepared and expect it, it won't surprise you when you realize you just may be having a bad relationship *day*, not a crisis. If you *worked hard to keep the traditions* going, then your road may not be as tough. If you let the traditions slide, it can still be corrected; it will just be more work. Traditions need to be maintained! Can you tell by now how important traditions are?

Marriage and family counseling can be a great option here as well. This option should be discussed well before you need it. Are you both willing to try this avenue if (when) your relationship with each or with the whole family is strained? I have learned that only men and women who are secure in themselves can admit when they need help. They generally have healthy egos and know they can't manage everything on their own. These people see counseling as an avenue of strength not weakness. If your relationship is in trouble, or your kids are adversely affecting it, or if problems in your relationship are adversely affecting your kids, find someone to help you sort things out.

You can't fix your transmission by yourself; you hire a professional.

You most likely wouldn't try to build your house without a contractor. Marriage is more difficult than both of those, so why should you and your partner be expected to do it without help from a professional?

Stage 6: Empty Nest Syndrome

This is the stage where you (or both of you) still work and your children want to be on their own, via college or their own apartment. Some couples get to this stage and realize that sex has become a rare event and maybe not that important—or maybe you just don't say anything. Companionship and friendship have often become the primary choice here. If you have let your sex fall to the side and want to rekindle, revisit the dating period. Start over!

You have a good understanding of your partner by this stage, so now it's your turn to *reconnect*. Put together a plan for this stage too. Do you want to take trips? Buy a smaller house and rehab it? Do you want to just sit back, stay home, and spend more time with friends? I have found the more time you spend reconnecting with your partner, the happier the two of you will be.

Here is a surprising example of how empty-nesters who spend a lot of time together can enjoy it and get along better if traditions and compatibility remain intact throughout the marriage. I had one family member and two friends whose partners lost their jobs, so they were unexpectedly home together (the partners worked at home). While the unemployed partners continued looking for work, they all commented that they were getting along better than when they were both working. They were all surprised by this. Suddenly they had time to be together as well as get things done around the house that they never had time to do before.

The unemployed partner also made life easier for the working partner, the house might get cleaned or dinner was ready when the other was done working. It was a good reminder to all of them that thoughtfulness and putting the time in to support each other is a good approach no matter how long you've been together.

The flip side to this is that after raising the children and ignoring each other for twenty years, the two, one-time newlyweds have grown apart. Your interests are not the same; you may want different things for your futures. This can happen if you didn't keep the partnership as a priority. Traditions, communication, and respect broke down.

If you feel yourselves start growing apart, revisit the traditions and start over with doing things together again. Take cooking or dance classes. Take on an interest that your partner developed while the children were growing up. Get season tickets to something you each like to do—like the theater and the game—or something you *both* like to do. Make sure you and your partner reciprocate here. Share each other's new interests.

Stage 7: Retirement!

By this time, you might say you probably made it. I have heard of couples who had adult children (age forty to fifty), married for fifty-plus years, and then they divorced. It still affected the adult children greatly. Maybe even more so because the children thought after fifty-some years of marriage, their parents were too old or set in their ways to get divorced. I guess their parents proved them wrong! For a friend of mine that this happened to, it was like facing a death. She had to learn that there would be no more holidays together with her parents, her kids' grandparents; everything was now to be dealt with separately. After that many years together, her parents were no longer going to attend family functions, parties, holidays, and all the special events together. My friend was really grieving.

That sad story is to tell you this: Take time to enjoy your life together. RECONNECT! Marriage is all about CONNECTION! Take trips together, even if it is only down memory lane. And I mean that literally. Think of the trips you made with your children. Now do that with just the two of you. If you made it this far, you should have many years of memories. Relive both the happy ones and the not-so-happy ones, except, this time correct the mistakes by making them all happy. This includes trips you may have taken to the zoo with the kids—remember how it wasn't all that much fun because it was chaotic? This time make it fun!

You will be surprised how many memories you have created, good and bad. This time you can work on making them all new, good, memories! Maybe you will even laugh about how silly your arguments were the first time you went to … wherever you went.

Most couples do have dreams about what they will do when they retire. Go live those dreams. If you had a relationship that took you this far, you have done a lot of work and should have a great sense of comfort with your partner. If you have maintained *your job* (relationship!), your partner knows you the best and probably loves you more than the day you got married because of all the shared life experiences.

That's what I've been told by those who are at that age anyway! I'm not old enough to know yet!

Chapter 6
Myths, Ideals & Fantasies of Marriage

People have lots of myths, ideals, and fantasies regarding marriage. These are usually based on your perception, fears, and dreams of marriage—or even simple cohabitation—but not based in reality or facts. The glamorized fairy tales, romantic movies and books are just what they claim to be: fiction. They are what someone's imagination wants or hopes can happen. If they are fairy tales, they can't happen, but if they are ideals, they can be something to work toward. But don't expect something wonderful to become a reality unless you are willing to do the work to make it happen.

Read on to see if any of these ideas sound familiar to you:

I'm holding out for the perfect partner.

There is no perfect partner because we are flawed by nature and can't achieve perfection. You might have an idea of your ideal relationship but you have to work for it. You don't *find* true love; you work at it until you get it.

This happened to me. When I first met my second husband. I wasn't sure I even liked him. He wasn't my *ideal* of the perfect man. The more I got to know him, however, the more I saw the qualities my first relationship was lacking. He was kind and respectful to everyone, with no judgments. He grew on me, and within a couple months, I realized I had grown to appreciate him. I "fell in love" with him, which grew to a deeper love. Fourteen years later, I can't imagine my life without him.

This is an example of letting love grow by showing up every day and staying open to what is really important. *No one* is perfect. You have flaws, your partner has flaws. Decide what *qualities* are really important to you—sit down and make a list (mentally or physically) of as many of them as you can, then make sure you have them yourself—and then find someone else who has those qualities too, keep in mind that looks and body image fade, personalities don't. Put the fairy tales away and see your partner for the wonderful qualities they possess, and then build a real relationship on that.

It can be fun to play house.

Think about this one! Is it really fun to work all day, only to come home to the dreaded question: *What do I make for dinner?*! Or worse, "What's for dinner?" There are many things that are not fun when playing house. You could create a tradition to help make the mundane chores more fun. I use to make a menu for the week (sometimes with my husband), so I knew what to purchase when I went grocery shopping. My husband would also want to cook some of the meals because we had a menu. Women have traditionally been saddled with this chore, but men are, thankfully, becoming more willing to help out with the cooking. It really takes pressure off that dreaded question, what to make for dinner!

Is it fun to have twice the laundry to drag to the Laundromat if you don't have a house or apartment that offers that option? *No, IT'S NOT.* Is it also fun to mow the lawn, make house repairs, clean, and all the other stuff that comes from *playing house*? *No, IT'S NOT.* A realtor once told me that people want to bring their X-Box not their toolbox to their new home. I thought that was funny, from the perspective of an interior designer. But it's true. I don't know anyone who truly enjoys doing maintenance on their homes or spending all weekend on yard work.

These aspects of playing house are not fun. They are necessary evils however! If you don't do your own maintenance or repairs, but must hire someone or ask your landlord to do it, that can be even more frustrating. You have to be home for the repairman, or strangers come in when you're not home, and that's after you get the go ahead and a repairman has been found. You have to spend the day waiting when you would rather be out doing something productive or fun. Ether one is better than waiting for someone who might not even show.

Home ownership is great because you have the freedom to do what you want, but it also includes a lot of work and a boatload of money, and these are necessary but not always fun. Know it and expect it and the work won't be such a shock. The earlier you lay down guidelines, traditions, or each person's role in any given task, it can become easier. It would depend on your attitude while doing these mundane, if not downright *evil* chores.

We know marriage is work, but we will <u>enjoy</u> the work.

Really! You might enjoy the work, it's true, but probably not until you've had years of knowing what to expect. Right out of the gate, however, not many people getting married understand the commitment or work they are about to undertake. Things like compromise, saving money, no malls, pasta five nights a week ... The only fun part about this is having the same goal. The excitement of saving for a house can be worth the pasta *seven* days a week. Working toward a common goal is always a good thing. Buying a house, taking a vacation, saving for something fun or a large toy like a boat or four-wheelers....

If you believe you will enjoy the work, then ask yourself and your partner: DO YOU ENJOY YOUR JOB EVERY DAY? I'm guessing your answer is no! You have good days at work, great days, and bad days; a lot of them are just ... *days*. Your relationship will be no different. If you can tell yourself that *Today was just a bad day, but I will make tomorrow a better day* ... and then if you can make it happen by remembering the *free* traditions, then you will have a handle on the process. Next, thank your partner for putting up with you on a bad day. Say "Thank you for letting me vent about work or my—fill in the blank—issues," and you will be surprised at how that changes your mood and your partner's. It has worked for me as well as others I have told this to.

He's my soul mate!

That's great that you are marrying your soul mate. Now, ask yourself what makes them your soul mate? If you enjoy doing everything together, is that a good thing? Of course, your answer is yes! But wait! Don't be so quick to say yes. It can get boring if you both enjoy the same things; what surprises does that leave you to look forward to? Sometimes it can be nice to enjoy *different* things; then you can learn about those interests from your partner. Trying new things is how we learn and grow.

Furthermore, what happens to your perceptions of your soul mate if one of you changes interests or matures differently or quicker than your partner? Yes, you will mature; different things will interest you at different stages. Expect it, and don't read into it that your partner doesn't want to spend time with you. Communicate your concerns to your partner. Stay flexible and enjoy *your* time and they can enjoy *their* time.

If you continue the date night tradition along with the other traditions, your interests may become diverse, but you can include your partner in your new interest and *discover* you both enjoy it. Again, remain flexible, be willing to try new things that interest your partner. You should also have interests that are different. Many happily married couples I interviewed said they enjoyed their time away from their partners. It gave them something new and maybe interesting to talk about.

For example, I know quite a few men *and women* who enjoy fantasy football. If your partner enjoys that, then while they are planning their season, you can use that time to do what you enjoy. I have yet to find anyone who wants to be with their partner 24/7, even if you are *soul mates*.

If you can both stay *flexible* and expect life to change as you mature, then your partner can still be your soul mate, even as you become less connected at the hip. All that's happened is that you have each matured and now understand that varied interests can be fun and an interesting addition to the relationship.

I will do whatever it takes to make my marriage work.

Here is a clear *ideal*, and I hope you will. *But* ... what makes you think you can? Do you understand the work and emotional investment involved? The struggles you will face with your own unwillingness to surrender, to compromise, and to know when to fight for the relationship and not get your way? Are you always completely honest with each other? Do you disagree fairly? Do you *never* argue? Do you both have a great sense of humor? Are you patient? Are you good with compromise? Are you upfront and honest with your partner?

I have never met anyone who has ever said, "I'm getting married so I can get divorced!" That would be crazy. No one ever plans on divorcing, yet it happens. Why?

I believe that a lot people entering into relationships or marriage have little understanding of the work involved only because they haven't been there yet. When you have a rough day in your relationship, remember this thought: If you have a rough day at work do you quit? No, you chalk it up to a bad day ... or week ... or year. You expect to have bad days at work. Why wouldn't you expect to have bad days in your relationship?

Relationships today are also more complex than they were fifty years ago. Both partners now work, there are more temptations with technology, and life's pace has gotten out of control. Understanding the way your partner reacts to different situations and why they react that way can be very helpful in helping you understand why they do the things they do. They handle situations, people, work, and so on in different ways.

It has been accepted that men are analytical, focused on thoughts, and women are emotional, focused on feelings. When you communicate with your partner it may be helpful to give your partner examples of what you are upset about. It's also a good idea to be clear and concise. Arguments are very emotional, so try and keep your emotions in check by walking away when you are finding yourself becoming irrationally emotional. That goes for both sexes. I know some men who are more emotional than some women and vice versa especially when an argument arises.

Understanding this, help your partner comprehend what you want by being very clear and concise. Be specific. If you understand where each partner is coming from, it might help you become more patient and understanding of your partner's viewpoint.

If you aren't aware of how the different sexes view things (emotionally or analytically) the little issues can grow into big issues until everything starts to annoy you about the person you once couldn't wait to marry. Remember *all* the men I worked with said, "I don't understand what my wife wants"? It really was sad because I could see how much they really wanted to make their partner happy, they just lacked the tools. And that's after years of marriage.

Both sexes want to be needed, appreciated, respected, treated kindly, and enjoyed for who they are—or might become. Can your partner be spontaneous? Can you and your partner respect the differences you have? Can you enjoy learning about those differences without judgment?

Having some different opinions and outlooks on things can make you a great couple. Learning is how we grow as humans. Problems will arise. Remember to try to handle them maturely, calmly, with kindness and respect. This will be very difficult to do sometimes!

The other side to this is if you and your partner never disagree. One or both of you may be agreeing because you aren't comfortable telling your partner the truth. People who tend to do this are called *enablers*. They enable dysfunctional behavior in their loved ones, which helps no one. They will agree just to avoid conflict. They don't want to upset their partner, they would rather frustrate themselves.

If you are being honest, and you still never disagree, the relationship may lack passion or emotion, according to some counselors I have spoken with. If you are agreeable to this lack of passion or emotion in the relationship, that's great. You will probably have a long marriage without too much drama or too many changes. You should have an even-keel relationship with no ups or downs. There is nothing wrong with that as long as you *both* know that about each other and accept it.

Do you try to make your partner feel better when they have had a rough day? Do you respect their feelings and take them seriously? It's critical that you do! That shows genuine caring for your partner. I'm not saying you have to *agree* with their feelings, but you do need to *respect their feelings!*

Remember: A long-lasting relationship is priceless! Divorce isn't!

We watch all those romantic comedies, and that's the life we're going to have!

Yes, you can have a fun life and marriage, but you have to *work hard*, compromise, and be able to realize that sometimes you will be wrong. Do you know the right words to say? Do you get upset easily? Can you laugh at yourself?

If you are able to laugh at yourself and realize how insignificant *small* arguments are, that can be helpful. Remember, the small stuff, if not addressed, will turn into big stuff. You should never use humor if it's a serious issue, your partner may (and should) get upset that you are not taking their issue seriously! If you can put the comedy in your romance, at the right time, diverting the impulse to whine and bicker with humor— you might just be lucky enough to have the marriage you want. By reading this book, I hope you will establish the foundation for that life.

Remember, you are marrying a human being; there really is no white horse and no prince, no sleeping beauty and no perfect kiss. There are no writers in the shadows feeding your partner the perfect words to say. We all wish there was, but that's fantasy not reality. Ask yourself: how many of the romantic leads, in real life, are happily married; how many times have they been divorced?

If you and your partner watch the romantic movies, where the guy always says the perfect lines, ask yourself, who wrote those lines? It was probably a team of people! Again, it's a myth and not reality. Some men are not innately romantic, but are realists or pragmatic (you remember, thinkers). They don't have writers telling them what to say. Be fair, realistic, and kind. If you are the romantic one in the relationship, lead by example if you want romance. Be romantic with your partner, and they will probably understand better what romantic means to you.

Romance also means different things to different people. Young men may offer *traditional* romantic answers, i.e. flowers, dinner, etc. An older man's idea of romance may be watching a TV program together, bringing you a blanket when you are cold.

A woman's idea of romance also varies as she ages and has been in the relationship longer. Newlyweds or young women may want the romantic-type man they see in movies. The perfect sweet words spoken at the perfect time. That's how my sisters, friends, and I felt when we were young.

If you ask a woman who has been married a while what romance means, her definition will be different, more realistic. She may say having her partner wash the dishes, make dinner, or even pick up their socks. Their expectations are more grounded in reality. See what you have to look forward to!

That is why each of you has to tell your partner *exactly* what you believe romance is. Be precise, in a short, clear message. Tell them you want flowers, or dinner reservations, a thoughtful card, a bath with candles, whatever your idea of romance is. A great exercise for this is to go buy those poetry magnets for your refrigerator—the ones with words on them. Put phrases together that tell your partner how you feel or what you want for that day or week. It can be romantic, funny, thoughtful, or simply a message of love. It really does help your partner understand what you want in a clear and precise way!

This works for both partners. You can even have one side of the fridge for you to put magnets on and another side for your partner. Make sure it's your idea of romance and not what you think your partner wants that you are spelling out. Reciprocity is important!

My husband's idea of an evening of romance, for example, is watching TV together. Whether it's a sporting event or movie! He says its romantic just to spend time together. I respect his feelings and happen to agree with him, but it's not everyone's idea of romance.

If I want him to say something romantic to me, I will be specific with him by even saying what I want him to say. I will ask him, "Can you say something sweet to me?" or say, "Tell me what you love about me." After a minute of thinking, he will say something that he considers sweet or kind. Even that may not be what I was hoping for, but if that is sweet to him and I can accept that answer, I will say, "Aww. Thank you!" Even then, if I don't feel it was romantic *enough*, I will tell him exactly want I want. An example may be "Tell me you think I'm—something nice"; then he can fill in the blank. Then I will reciprocate.

Sometimes, ladies and gentlemen, that is how *specific* you have to be to get what you want. Don't get upset if this is the case. Accept it and appreciate the effort. Eventually, he may do this on his own, but if not, then just keep giving him examples of exactly what you want. Behavior modification works! Think: *positive reinforcement!* You may have to do this for weeks, months, or years. Don't get discouraged. Be realistic. Remember aim low; avoid disappointment. *Never expect your partner to read your mind, and don't try to read theirs; it's not fair and very unrealistic.*

My partner can make me happy ...

Now, that would be fantasy not reality. If you aren't a happy person to begin with, no one can make you happy but yourself. I spent a lot of years learning that this is true. Your partner can only enhance your happiness if you are already happy. If you are someone who likes to complain, sees the glass half empty, and lives for drama in your life, you may have past issues that you have not resolved. You will bring that into your relationship and, more than likely, put those issues on your partner, making them put up with your issues. That's not fair! Be aware of that.

Everyone has *baggage* they bring to a relationship. My husband brought his. He had unresolved issues with his neglectful childhood. He grew up taking care of himself since he was fourteen. When you have a trauma like that, you can get stuck at that age level unless you resolve those issues through any variety of therapeutic methods. Since I was aware of that, I could also understand that his issues didn't have to be my issue. So when he felt he had to do everything by himself and never ask for help, I recognized it as part of his past trauma. I have been helping him work through those issues patiently since 1999. He has a great heart, so I felt he was worth the work. Plus, I understand where it comes from, so I have never taken it personally. He can now ask for help on some tasks— after fourteen years of building trust and receiving constant positive reinforcement when he asks me for help. My point here is, don't expect transformations in your partner's behavior to happen quickly!

I can change him.

Oh, I hear this quite often, and it is a huge myth! I also believe that if you feel you need to change your partner, then they are not the one for you. If your partner is uncomfortable communicating—especially feelings— they probably won't be good at communicating during the long term. It's not that they don't want to; they just may not understand how to!

If they enjoy too much alcohol, it probably won't get better after marriage. If the partner is *very sensitive*, they will probably always be that way. If your partner is insecure or has low self-esteem, they will probably always have those issues., and so on.

Trying to change someone to fit your *ideal* of what your partner should be is arrogant. It can affect their self-esteem and change their attitude toward you down the road. Women, I find, are more guilty of this than men. I know one man who tired of his wife nagging him to change, so he left her.

Changing small issues is something different. Here is the good news: They are learned behaviors that have now become embedded in their personality. Behavior modification (to modify one's behavior) can help soften your partner's learned personality traits but not eliminate them. For example, if your partner is shy, the more they practice socializing and get praise from their partner, the less shy they may become—but they will still be shy. If they are inconsiderate, you can thank them every time they do something considerate, no matter how small their gesture was and they may learn what considerate means—but still may not be as considerate as you would like. Again, the point is you can, *maybe*, change small annoyances and slightly lessen particular traits, but don't count on it without professional intervention.

Here is a simple way to modify small annoyances. Everyone likes to be told "Good job!" or "I like the way you did that," etc., so praise your partner for doing something well or thoughtful, be patient and kind. If they are overly sensitive, *by your definition*, it might modify (not change) or soften, but only if you encourage good decisions, not by fighting about them.

Here is a concrete example of how behavior modification can work. My husband was never good at grilling. I used to *tell* him to ask someone (That was my first mistake; try not to *tell* your partner to do anything, but suggest or ask them to), like our butcher or our friend who was great at grilling to show him how they grilled their steaks. *Big mistake*—he felt I was berating his grilling style, so he just stopped grilling.

The following grill season I decided to use *positive reinforcement* when it came to his grilling. The first five or six times, his steaks were still over-cooked, tough or too rare. Instead of making him feel inadequate as a griller, I simply said thank you and lied about how good it was. He knew it wasn't good (men have taste buds too), but he felt proud that I was willing to eat it. Then he adjusted his cook time and even asked the butcher for ideas. And now I'm sincere when I say his steaks are good!

If you tell someone they did a good job and thank them for doing it, they will usually continue trying to improve upon their results. This technique is great and necessary for maintaining a happy relationship. It's a win–win for both partners and easy to do if you just remember to say thank you *every time* your partner does something, anything, for you. Remain positive.

Here is what can happen when you *don't* show appreciation for your partner's attempts: One of my sisters used to tell her husband that he couldn't do the laundry right. He wouldn't add the right amount of soap, or he added water before the clothes were loaded or vice versa. It wasn't *her* way, so in her eyes it wasn't done right. Guess what eventually happened? Yep, he stopped doing laundry. Now, she has to do all the laundry herself!

If you don't reward or praise your partner for a good job, or for at least trying, they will more than likely stop trying, which you can hope remains confined to the area you criticized rather than expanding to the relationship itself, but isn't it better not to risk that? Try this: praise your partner often and watch the change in their behavior!

Your partner can modify their own behavior with help from you, but it does require knowledge of how behavior modification works. Make sure you are honest with yourself—and your partner—about what personality traits you can and cannot live with. Habitual behavior can be modified, but it's important to get that *you can't change your partner.* Can you live with the behavior the rest of your life?

We can work through the bad times because we love each other.

In marriage, it really does take more than love to work through the bad times. It takes open communication, trust, patience and honesty. Marriage is about companionship and a partnership more than anything, in my opinion. Let's say you have chosen someone whom, you believe, will be by your side when the going gets tough. He or she will have your back. Your partner has realistic expectations that marriage is work but is still willing to work on it with you.

You need to discuss what both *happiness* and "*bad times* mean to you individually and as a couple. How will you work through them? What happens if you suffer a financial crisis? What happens if one of you gets sick? How do you know you will stand by your partner? These are very tough questions to answer. Sometimes you don't know how you will handle a situation until it arises. If this happens, stay flexible and remember professional help is an option. Are you both willing to seek outside help when the going gets tough?

Here is something that happened in my relationship and how I handled it. I became disabled, and my life, as well as my partner's life, drastically changed. We had both been athletic, worked out six days a week, and played sports together. I taught downhill skiing, went dancing with my friends and shopping with my daughter. I can no longer do any of that.

It was a very drastic lifestyle change. I thought for sure that was the end of the marriage. Why would he stay? Can he handle a slower life style? We went to marriage counseling so we could better understand what we were *both* going through. We went to strengthen our marriage and get help with the enormous lifestyle changes we were facing. I learned that my husband was just as affected by my disability as I was. I was only focused on my physical pain and had forgotten about his emotional pain.

I soon realized that if your partner is in pain (physical or emotional), you will also feel pain. We had a good marriage before my disability; now it's a *great* marriage, thanks to help from counseling. I do believe marriage counseling—with a good counselor—should happen in every marriage, whether the marriage is good or bad.

He went through the grieving process with me, and we both realized that the most important thing in marriage was to have someone who really "hung in there" through the bad times. It was a tough adjustment for both of us, but now we both feel it brought us closer, because we were forced to change our priorities. We found out that *we* are what's important, not the things we did.

There are times when I watch people who are always busy, active, and sociable. I watch them and sometimes feel jealous, but soon I realize that they are in a lifestyle that I no longer envy. They are so busy with their activities and their own lives they forget how important it is to have time for their partner and the simple times you can spend together, watching a movie, playing games, or just talking.

Chapter 7
Creating a Plan

So far, we have discussed stages of relationships and myths. If you are moving toward a commitment, you will need a concrete plan of what will be expected in your new job called marriage.

Discuss—before you move in together—what your duties are going to be around the house. This may sound stupid or odd, but it works. Be very clear at this point. Both partners need to be involved. It's important that you participate whether you want to or not. Don't leave the "relationship stuff" up to one partner. That's not fair, and it also shows a low level of commitment to your partner.

Here are some examples of how clear or specific you need to be when establishing a plan.

1. Household Chores

- Do you both recycle?
- Who is in charge of the recycling and returning cans (if that applies)?
- Who will take the dry cleaning in?
- Who will pick it up?
- Who is doing what part of cleaning the house, mowing the lawn, etc.
- Who does the grocery shopping; who makes the list, etc., etc., etc.!

If you decide together how the chores will be divided and get done, it will be more equitable. Whatever you can establish in the early stage, the more it becomes routine and arguments averted. If one partner puts in fewer hours at work than the other, for example, that partner should be willing to take on a few more responsibilities at home-in my opinion. Just stay fair and flexible to changes.

Have a contingency plan. You can expect different chores to come up at different times. Who will be in charge of hiring help, if you own a house, and the faucet leaks; who will oversee construction work on the house? Who will be in charge of finding, hiring, and paying the babysitters if you have children? Whatever you do, the important thing to remember is to know what to expect and have a plan to meet what comes. It can be verbal or written, whatever you decide. Just stick to the plan.

One couple I interviewed have been married twenty-seven years. They attribute some of their success to dividing up the chores around the house—from day one. The resentments they've avoided are apparent! They have always shared household-cleaning duties. One week she cleans the upstairs while he does the downstairs; the next week, they rotate. She always does the laundry, and he always mows the lawn or shovels snow.

On hard days of work, she calls her husband to let him know she doesn't want to cook that day early enough for him to bring something home for them. If she doesn't call early enough, then at the very least, he knows they will be ordering out. They are very good at *staying flexible*.

This kind of plan can prevent many arguments down the road. It can also be another tradition that you establish so you both know what is expected. The more you know what is expected of this union, the fewer surprises.

2. Finances

Having different ideas about money and how it is used is one of the top reasons for divorce. Agree, early and clearly, on how finances will be handled *before* you move in together or get married. You should discuss how each other views spending.

- Is one a saver and the other a spender?
- Are you both spenders?
- Did you have to deal with finances growing up or did your parents take care of everything?

- *Be honest and open* about how much debt you are coming into the relationship with.
- Who is responsible for debts prior to your marriage (credit card debt, school loans, past child support, liens, etc.)?

Like everything else, it comes down to communication. If you can discuss openly and honestly the way you both feel about money/bills/debts and other expenses, you will have a better understanding of your partner's experience with finances.

Here are the three top examples of systems that people I've spoken to have had success with. Perhaps one of them will work for your relationship.

A. She has her money; he has his money, and then you have a household fund. The household fund is for the mortgage, utilities, taxes, groceries, household repairs, birthdays, Christmas, insurance, and miscellaneous expenditures. One partner uses this fund to pay all the bills. You can decide who that will be. It is also important to find equitable percentages, based on your individual incomes, to contribute to the general fund. For example, If your bills come to $2,400.00 a month, and one makes $10k and the other makes $2k, then you each put in 20% of what you take home. Whatever is left out of your paychecks goes into your personal accounts for whatever you need. The one with the higher income will obviously put in more, but more will also be left over.

B. You divide up the bills, deciding together—again, based on how much you each make—who pays what bills. This may be the most common method if your salaries are comparable. One may pay the mortgage, while the other pays the utilities and taxes. You want to make sure this way is equitable to both partners as well. When it comes to household items, daily expenses like groceries or home repairs, that needs to be worked out. You can use a general fund that both people add to each pay period or decide who pays for the groceries and who buys presents. People I spoke with tended to split the groceries and all the extras like presents, repairs and maintenance, etc. Some couples start a Christmas fund through work or at their bank. They both add to it each pay period. You could also start a miscellaneous fund for presents, parties, dinners out, household repairs, etc., that you both add to each pay period. Again, just make sure it is equitable to both partners.

You can also take care of your own families of origin for birthdays and such. This may or may not be fair if one of you has a large family and the other doesn't. Keep that in mind when you work out the expenses.

C. The old-school method has become less common, believe it or not. That's when you pool all your money into one, joint account. This is the least productive way, in my experience, as it can lead to arguments about every dime spent, and it's the least equitable.

For this method to work, you need to really trust each other. The partner selected to pay everything *must* be good at budgeting. The other partner needs to trust that the bills are all getting paid. You have to trust that your partner isn't overspending on things that you didn't agree to. If one gives their paychecks to the other, then only one partner is doing all the financial work. That can be a lot of responsibility for you or your partner. If something happens, and you fall short one month on a bill, that partner is going to be the one to take the blame when it might not be their fault. There are always extra expenses when you own a home or decide to have children, and one partner might not have access to the money when needed.

That happened in my first marriage. It was a real bone of contention, because it was always my fault when we were short. Some months I would have five birthdays to buy for and that would short our budget. If we would've talked (at least monthly) about our budget, he would've had a better understanding of where the money was going. We did not discuss finances until it was too late.

Let's discuss allowances for a moment. This means each of you draws some spending money out of the budget each week. You may think this sounds stupid or disempowering, but it can be the opposite. Once married, you should both be living in the same socioeconomic class, but one of you might make considerably less than the other. Since you will both need money for coffee, lunches, gas, extras, and so on, an equal allowance gives you both the same financial freedom—or restrictions without getting you caught up in the credit card game. Make sure the money you decide on is enough to cover extras that might come up. A rule of thumb suggests 10% of your budget will, more than likely, be spent on miscellaneous items. You should budget for that in your allowances.

This is a difficult way to do things if only one person in the relationship knows where the money is going. When one partner all of a sudden needs money and the money holder doesn't have it, accusations of mismanagement start getting thrown around. Then the one controlling the money becomes defensive and resentful that their partner doesn't trust them when they say there just is no money.

This can be a very good way to handle finances, however, if one partner is better at budgeting and managing money than the other. If one of you grew up with a silver spoon in their mouth, asking for whatever they wanted and getting it, and the other has been pinching pennies since childhood, learning well how to stretch a dollar into next week, then you're going to handle money very differently. If your budget is slim and that silver-spooner sees a dollar and spends it, then that penny pincher is the best bet to hold the purse strings.

This has happened in a few relationships I know. One person grew up with parents who handed them everything so they expected to get what they wanted once they got married. That is usually not realistic, because you may want to save for a house, vacations, the kids' education, or maybe just meeting monthly bills is difficult. If this is your situation, I recommend that the partner who learned how to budget take over the paychecks and give their partner spending money every pay period. For this situation, it can help avoid a lot of frustration on both partners. If it doesn't work, you can always modify the finances until you find a plan that works for both of you.

If you both agree to leave it up to only one partner, then you will have to live with those choices. It takes trust that your partner is paying the bills, understands budgeting, and when they say there is no money, than there isn't. That's where the trust and communication on a weekly or at least monthly basis *are essential*.

Some men I have interviewed like it when the women handle the finances, so they don't have to be bothered. This is only a good idea if one partner excels at budgeting and the other doesn't. You may end up arguing, like my friends, over where every dollar goes and that starts the blame game!

If you *do* spend time with the blame game, then agree to sit down and work through to a compromise. Change the way you handle the finances. *If the one doing the "blaming" isn't willing to take responsibility for their finances, then let them know that they can't complain about something they aren't willing to change!*

***

Whichever way works for you in finances, make sure you both agree and can live with it. Remember that nothing is set in stone. If you thought one way would work and it doesn't—*stay flexible and change it.*

If you choose any of these strategies or choose one of your own, it's important to have discussions every pay period or month (maybe on date night) so you both understand where the money is going. You can modify the finances as needed. I say on date night because it will be uninterrupted conversation, in public, like a restaurant, so neither party will get upset. If the topic is too heated to stay calm, don't do this on a date night—they are intended to be fun!

Here is an example of how important it is to agree on finances: A friend of mine told me that his wife had never had to worry about money because her parents took care of all her financial needs up until she married. Now she expects her husband to do the same. She works but hands him her paycheck. He had to work for everything and has learned how to budget. He tries to take care of all the money.

His wife has no idea how much money they have—or *don't* have. She, therefore, still wants what she wants and gets very angry if she can't have the trips, clothes, or whatever she thinks she needs. But she didn't want to take any responsibility—or maybe didn't know how—so she shouldn't blame her partner when she can't afford something. The tension might have been resolved by giving her an allowance so she could take responsibility for her own money.

I suggested to my friend that he and his partner sit down and come up with a better financial plan, including the idea that she pay some of the bills out of her money and he pay some of the bills out of his money. That way, if she over spent, she couldn't blame him. He was not willing to do that—he didn't want to give up control—so whose fault is it really? Another reason communication is so important in every relationship.

A financial planner once told me that *both* parties need to be involved in the finances in the case of illness, divorce or premature death. If only one person handles everything and something happens, the other partner won't know about the life insurance, mutual funds, banking, or other important information. I have seen this happen, and *oh, what a mess.*

3. Children

Whether to have children is a very personal decision and also a very important one. If you both agreed that you want children, you should discuss shared (or unshared) values, belief systems, and educational goals and methods. It is very important to be on the same page *before* you get married. It can be a casual conversation, but at least you will both have an idea of the way your partner is thinking,

Child-rearing can create a great amount of stress on your relationship. You should discuss this in depth before you get married. It's a very serious subject that can make or break a relationship.

- Do you want children?
- If so, how many?
- Is adoption an option?

These can be straight-forward questions that you don't have a hard time with as a couple. Either you do or you don't. Or it could be a tough question: one of you does, and one of you doesn't; one of you does, and the other isn't sure because she or he expects to be the one who does most of the responsible parenting and doesn't want that. Whatever it is, remember nothing is set in stone, and things can change (though if that's what you're hoping for, you need to go back and reread the bulleted item "I can change my partner" in the previous chapter).

If you have decided you *don't* want children, you should discuss what will happen if one of you changes your mind and decides you do want them. Is your partner flexible or open-minded enough to talk about revisiting it? If you both feel you are compatible in almost every way but this one, you need to have a hard conversation: Is there any hope of one of you changing your mind? If one wants children and the other doesn't, find out why. Can you both spend time with your siblings' or friends' babies to get a feel for the reality?

This is also a situation that can happen: You both agree that you don't want kids. My brother and sister-in-law said (even after they got married) that they weren't having children. Two years later, something changed in both of them. She got pregnant, had a boy, and two years later, had another boy. We were all surprised, because they always insisted they weren't having children. Now they can't imagine life without their sons!

If you both decide you want to have children, before you get married you should discuss your beliefs on how they should be raised. I stress *before* you get married, because once you have a child, you will be under the *love-is-blind* spell. You will become so engrossed in your infant that your belief systems are overtaken by love.

This was a very stressful time for my first husband and me. We had never discussed how we were going to raise our children. As a teacher, I believed that children should work for the things they wanted. I would have them do extra chores for the money and then take them shopping for the things they'd earned. My husband, an only child, was given everything, so he wanted that for our children. This led to many arguments that became insurmountable.

These are some questions you should ask yourself and your partner regarding children:.

- What types of *correction* method do you feel comfortable with?[1]
- Are there religious beliefs to resolve?
- Are you both patient?
- Do you think reading books can help?
- Do you want kids to work for what they want or get it because they are a member of the family and do chores?

I'm sure this will lead to your own thinking process about children based on your own childhoods. But once you decide you both want kids, it's important to share your thinking processes with each other *before* you get married and before you get pregnant.

4. Plan on things happening that you can't plan for

In all relationships things can pop up that you couldn't foresee-therefore-no plan.

---

1   I prefer *correction* to *discipline*. It is more accurate.

- What happens if you get a job transfer?
- One wants to further their education?
- Can you support each other if something changes?

These are questions that are almost impossible to answer until faced with the decisions. I wrote them however, to keep in the back of your mind or a casual conversation about "what if…". Situations will arise that you can't plan for. Are you flexible enough to roll with the changes?

When you are developing and discussing your plans you should also consider time frames. What time frame would you want to buy a house, start a family, where do you both want to live. You may have your own time frame for other areas as well, make sure you discuss those as well.

Chapter 8
Ways to Compromise

The ability to compromise is a strong determinant with regard to compatibility. This is the ability to find a middle ground that is mutually agreeable to both partners. *If you are to be successful in your relationship, you can expect your relationship to be filled with compromise.* Every successful couple understands the importance of this! Don't ever expect to have it your way all the time! Find that middle ground, and take turns with whatever is applicable.

Take turns on leisure events.

If you like basketball and your partner likes car racing take turns doing these things or watching them, even if you don't enjoy their event. If you like ballet and your partner likes opera, take turns! Yes, I am avoiding stereotypes to make a point: the important thing to remember is to *take turns! You may even grow to enjoy your partner's interests.*

Take an interest in something that is important to your partner.

It's a sign that shows you care about your partner and their interests. Make sure there is reciprocity here, it can lead to resentment if your partner doesn't reciprocate with watching or doing something that interests you.

I told you the hockey story in a previous chapter. Well, it was true for NASCAR as well. As I mentioned, I learned to love watching professional hockey, though I'm still not overly excited about NASCAR. But I sit and do other things in the TV room with my husband while he watches the race.

Really, I pretend to watch, but I know enough to be able to talk about "our" drivers and what happened in their crashes. Reciprocally, my husband will pretend to watch HGTV or DIY with me! He will even comment sometimes on how nice a room looks or suggest we do that with our house. And just as I learned about hockey, he learned that there is more than one way to do things to a house. That's a good give-and-take in a relationship.

Alternate your likes and dislikes.

If one of you wants to vacation at a ski resort and the other loves basking in the sun, compromise. Go skiing where it's also sunny like Colorado or Utah. The following year, go somewhere warm at a place that has a lot to do. Most warm-weather resorts offer lots of options like parasailing or scuba diving.

Alternate with the little things too. Most of us can't afford to take turns with vacations—especially starting out. So, if your partner likes bowling and you like miniature golf, take turns.

If you also enjoy the same activities but at different levels, *compromise*. My husband and I like to gamble (not serious gambling); at different levels. He would like to go for hours and I don't. We compromise by going to a casino (only when we can afford it), never use the ATM, and only stay for one to two hours, tops. It's a nice compromise, because I keep his spending in check and he still gets to gamble within our agreed boundaries. We put a cap on the money we spend.

If you find your partner unwilling to compromise, then the next paragraph is good for you and your partner to read!

This is what can happen if you aren't willing to compromise on how some things should get done. My husband was not willing to compromise on the way I hung our Christmas lights. He wanted them done his way. He felt his way was better than my way for a variety of reasons. Since we were not able to compromise and do lights my way one year and his way the next year, he now does all the Christmas lights, every year.

This can be frustrating to the person who is unwilling to compromise. If you are that type of person, be prepared for the consequences. You may have to take on more duties—and you should not be resentful of your partner. You created the conditions by being unwilling to compromise.

I firmly believe in the saying "Be careful what you wish for!" For the reason above, I hope you understand how important compromise is.

Chapter 9
Types of Communication

Communication Issues in Relationships

The basic nature of the person is most apparent while he or she is in communication with others. The logical or emotional aspect of a person's personality not only dominates his or her perceptions, but also tings the style of talking. It takes the following forms:

- Passive
- Aggressive
- Assertive

Passive: Using passive communication, you tend to give priority to the welfare of others over yours. This results in creating the impression that you have a low self-image. Your voice is soft and tentative, giving your speech an apologetic note. Your body language, or nonverbal communication, is full of excessive head nodding, a stooped posture, eye-contact avoidance to the point of looking down or away as if you are searching, unsuccessfully, for some clues to advance the conversation out of thin air.

Is this form of communication harmful? Yes, it is! Using passive communication, you do everything in a conversation but express yourself, which is the heart of the conversation. It erodes your self-esteem and confidence and makes you angry at yourself. It earns you pity and disrespect from your partner! And you want respect!

Aggressive: The antithesis of the passive style expresses, "I am okay; you are *not* okay." The practitioner of an aggressive communication style is very much aware of what is good for him. However, he or she is not very particular about who gets hurt while they are achieving it. Your voice is loud and lets others know how superior you think you are. Nonverbal communication or body language takes an aggressive stance. The clenched tight fist, rigid body posture, and staring eyes are enough to intimidate the other individual. Adopting this style of communication is a sure-shot way of earning anger and disrespect from others.

Assertive: The best among all the types, this style is very conducive to healthy relationships. You can employ an assertive style by drawing from the various other communication styles to nourish and cement them. Your attitude speaks of the "You are okay, I am okay", approach. You value the rights of the individual you are in a relationship with, but not at the cost of your own. Your communication bestows importance and equal status to others and signifies a refusal to trample each other in any conversation. "Both of us can win", is your message to your partner, "by fulfilling our part of the bargain.". Communication in a relationship based on this style can lead to open, non-threatening communication.

Knowing this, you can determine which style you and your partner may use. The following breaks it down for you.

Face-to-Face communication

Verbal Communication

This is the most common style you will use in the relationship (I hope!). If you are talking to your partner, it's important to do this face to face for a few reasons.

First, the *way* things are said are just as important as what is said. Your partner's tone may indicate how they are feeling. Are the intonations funny, serious, concerned, etc.?

Second would be *how* they are said. Are they loud, talking fast, sound like they are confused? These also indicate how they are feeling. Talking loud can imply anger, impatience, frustration, or excitement. Or their ears could just be stopped up. Talking quickly can imply nervousness, anxiety, stress, or discomfort.

Body Language

Body language is also a very important communication tool that can only be observed face to face. Sometimes how things are said are more important than what is actually said. An example would be someone looking around while you are talking; that shows a lack of respect boredom or an uneasiness about the topic!

Does their body language suggest that they are open to communication? Do they maintain eye contact or do they continue watching the television or staring off into space while you are talking? They may *not* be interested in talking at that moment because they are tired or frustrated about something totally unrelated to you—so ask them *if they feel like listening,* if it has to be said at that moment or wait for a later time when they aren't frustrated.

Body language can give you more clues into how the partner is feeling. Do they usually walk with confidence but are slouching and look tired today? That may imply they are really just tired or that they've had a bad day. This would be a good time to ask how their day was. If they don't want to talk, ask if there is something else you can do to perk them up. If they still say no thank you; then drop it. Sometimes they will just appreciate that you noticed! This shows your partner that you know them and care. Who doesn't appreciate that? Respect and trust that if your partner doesn't want to talk, don't force it. You can make their day worse by forcing them to discuss their day, which only adds to their aggravation or frustration.

Respect that posture; it speaks volumes.

Rolling the eyes is also a form of body language. It says, "I don't really respect or believe what you are saying." Does your partner roll their eyes when you are talking? If they do, then stop the conversation and ask them if they aren't interested in the conversation. Try avoid starting your statement with *why* they rolled their eyes, it makes them defensive immediately. If they can't answer you, or deny they were rolling their eyes let them know what *eye-rolling* says to you and how it makes you feel. Wait for a response and then resume the conversation. If they don't respond, let them know you will bring up your conversation later—giving your partner time to digest the conversation. Sometimes rolling the eyes is a defensive strategy, because your partner has no idea how to answer your question or is uncomfortable with the conversation.

I have not included texting as a form of communication in your relationship because I strongly feel it's *not* one. Where is the body language? Where is the intonations of the message? Can you see their eyes rolling? Can you *hear* how they are feeling? Yes, you can add smiley faces, which may be helpful, but you need to *hear* what is being said when it's something important! Texting, in my opinion, should only be used for messages, *hence text message!*

Email is an okay way to communicate, but again, nothing important. Email is usually used for information and not intimate discussions. I have heard of people breaking up via email and text—that's a chicken's way out! Everyone deserves to know what went wrong, so they can learn and apply changes to the next relationship! It's also a great show of disrespect for someone you once cared about.

There are also physical gestures to express communication. No, I'm not referring to hand gestures, because they never communicate anything worth reacting to. I am more referring to gifts, tokens of appreciation, cards, notes. These are other ways to communicate your feelings or intentions. If you are a nervous, shy type or maybe insecure about how your partner feels, these gestures are a safe, non-confrontational way to get your point across. If they respond to your gesture the way you were hoping, it will give you more confidence to raise the level of communication!

Even though the whole process of communication may seem so simple, the effectiveness of each type depends to a great extent on how you interpret what your partner is or is not saying. If the conversation is unclear to you, then ask your partner to rephrase. Don't feel embarrassed or stupid if you didn't understand the first time; the important factor is to make you understand it, regardless of the repetition. You can also repeat what your partner said, back to them, and ask, "Is that what you meant? I didn't understand, and I really want to."

Good communication requires trust in your partner, respect for your feelings and thoughts, and knowing how to say what you want in a productive way. That is a challenge for today because people are more comfortable with texting than talking! Can you tell your partner anything? If not, why can't you? Do you trust your partner will listen? Can you tell your partner how you feel? *You must be able to communicate!*

Chapter 10
Games People Play

Men and women are very different in how they communicate. But saying what you mean and meaning what you say are not gender-specific. When people conceal their motivations and try to manipulate others' into doing what they want or taking responsibility for someone else's feelings, it can be called a *mind game*. I detest game playing, yet I see it daily. These games can ruin a relationship because it promotes manipulation of your partner! Sometimes people play these games in order to communicate their frustration in the relationship. It is the worst way to communicate, because it doesn't involve thoughtfulness for the partner, but rather exploits their weaknesses (aggressive communication). Both partners do this, but my experience indicates that women tend to be more guilty of game playing.

Instead, play a *good* learning game with your partner. See how many *feeling* words your partner can come up with in ten seconds. My guess is that men will come up with words like *anger* and *mad*, love, and then pause, at a loss for more. Women, on the other hand, may be able to come up with quite a few in ten seconds. If my theory is correct—and when I tested the theory, men came up with an average of two or three words—then women, you should have a clearer understanding of how difficult emotional understanding is for men, so give them a break. Help them find accurate words for how they feel.

I work in a man's world of construction, and a lot of the men don't understand what their partner is trying to say or what they want. I hear the same thing from every man: "I don't know why she is mad at me" or "I don't know what she wants me to do!" There is definite frustration in their voices, because, they admitted to me, they want to make their partners happy, but they just don't understand how. I felt bad for them, because I could tell how much they really wanted to do the *right thing;* they just didn't know what that was.

That's why women need to go by the KISS philosophy—Keep It Simple, Silly—when communicating with their partners. Here are some games you should not be playing:

The Guessing Game #1

Don't make your partner guess *what* you want or expect. Each of you is responsible for finding out what's important to you and then telling your partner in as concise a manner as you can. You should never expect anyone to read your mind. That is what I call *the guessing game.*

It is critical to help your partner out when it comes to understanding what you need or expect. If they tend to forget things that are important to you, next time, tell them that an important date is coming up in a few days and exactly why it's important. It may not register to your partner how important something is. Tell your partner what you want them to do or get to prepare for that date. That way, you won't be disappointed and your partner won't feel stupid for not realizing how important that date was!

For example, don't assume (ass of u and me) your partner knows when your birthday or anniversary is approaching. They might, for example, know the date but not be paying attention to the calendar to know that it's coming up next week. Tell them it's your birthday or anniversary next week or, better yet, *Thursday.* Be that specific.

Don't make them guess what to get you; tell them what you want just like you did with your parents when you were little. You might not think it's romantic now, but after a few years your partner might have learned what you like. Make sure you reciprocate as well! Men always seem to get the short end of the stick here!

The Guessing Game #2

"You should know how I feel" is another kind of guessing game, and that is just crazy. I must admit I played this game in my late teens and early 20s. I wouldn't tell my boyfriend and then husband when I was upset. I believed that he should know how I felt based on my body language! That guessing game is unrealistic. *Your partner can't read your mind!* This is also not a good idea, because it can set both of you up for disappointment, anger, and frustration.

Do try and avoid words like *mad, angry* or *pi**ed off*. These words are not concrete enough. Instead of mad you may try *annoyed*. Instead of angry try *upset*. The more specific you can be, the better. Try to use descriptive words that call attention to your feelings rather than an accusation. Words like upset, frustrated, confused, worried, nervous, anxious, and so on. These words tend to be less threatening. For example, I don't tell my husband that I'm mad, I try to say things like, "I feel frustrated when you don't ..." or "I get nervous when you drive because ..." (driving seems to be a big issue with everyone I have spoken to).

If your partner upsets you, *don't pout* about it like a child. Communicate like a real adult. If you have chosen the right person, you should be able to tell your partner anything and still feel secure in the fact that he/she still loves and respects you. Pouting or holding it against them only builds resentment and sets you up to play the victim. If the person you are with is victimizing you, leave the room, don't pout. When you calm down, go back and tell him/her what they did and offer solutions on how to make it better. Be concrete! Apologize for pouting!

My first husband used to say, "Can't you just be nice?"

That used to drive me crazy, and I would ask him "When aren't I nice ... and what do you mean by *nice*?"

His answer was "Ya know, just be *nice*."

I really never figured out exactly what he meant. If he could have given me an example of my being *not nice* or been clearer about what he wanted from me, it would have helped me greatly. It was a game, though, and not meant as clear communication.

The Clue Game

Maybe you think giving your partner clues should be enough. It can be fun, but only if you both know you are playing it. Don't hold a secret hope they picked up on some clue you dropped. Some people are very concrete. Are clues exact or concrete? No! Tell your partner exactly what you're thinking and what you need, want, or expect from them. Trust that your partner really *does* want to make you happy, and help them do so by not playing games.

Be fair. A lot of the clue game revolves around birthdays, holidays, anniversaries. You will need to tell them a few days before your birthday or anniversary, what you want to do or what you want. If you and your partner like games, make sure it's a game where you both win. Leave your partner word magnets or Post-its around the house that you are sure they will see. The note should be very clear. It may say "Birthday is Monday," "I love gift cards from (name of store)," or "I love the .... at (store)." You are telling your partner what you want and where to get it. They can surprise you if you give them two choices. Don't forget to reciprocate when it's your partner's birthday! Ask them what they want!

The Blame Game

The blame game often comes down to one partner saying "You never told me that," and the other saying "You never listen to me"!

So you should avoid the blame game at all costs. No one ever wins! If your partner didn't hear you, say it again. Explore the issues beneath what you are blaming each other for; break it down as clearly as you can. Find out why you feel the need to blame your partner. Both parties can be equally guilty of this. To avoid this game, make eye contact or at least be in the same room! I have yelled for my husband to grab something while in the basement and he's on the first floor. He didn't hear me-so who's fault is that?

A lot of the game can be about something insignificant too! Blaming your partner for misplacing something can be frustrating. Are you sure it was your partner? You can calmly ask them if they saw it. It's also helpful to be organized so everything has a place.

Partners do this quite often. Your partner might blame you for running out of food supplies (milk or bread), while you are blaming your partner for not telling you that you were out of milk. Okay, so you didn't look and your partner forgot. Don't blame each other, just go out and get more bread, or ask your partner to pick it up tomorrow!

Other blaming to avoid, if possible, include "why can't you ..." or "you never ..." (put the toothpaste cap on, replace the toilet paper, etc.). Speaking this way is bound to push your partner's buttons, throwing them into a child–parent role. You won't be having a conversation with your grownup partner; you'll be scolding a partner like a child, and they will be trying to get out of trouble. That is very unproductive!

Don't use words like *never* and *always*—they are instant agitators. If you do use those words intentionally, then you need to ask yourself what's really going on with *you*, and not your partner. Why would you intentionally use destructive words?

You might avoid that by saying what you need to once: "Would you put the cap on the toothpaste when you are done please? It dries out when the cap isn't on." Don't just blame them. Explain why you want something done a certain way. And if it drives you crazy, you could also just do it yourself. Remember, they are not your child and you don't want to be their parent; you want a grownup partner. Grownups do things in different ways. Blaming does not allow for that.

Look at them when you ask them, so you know they are listening. If you are honest and direct and tell them how much it frustrates you, you may have a better chance of success. If you need to bump the importance another level, you could say, "I feel disrespected, like my time is not valuable when you don't ... (fill in the blank)." That might get them to pay closer attention!

You are partners and teammates; remember that. When one falls down, the other helps to pick up the slack. These seemingly small annoyances can build into larger resentments if you don't keep them in check. Remember: honesty over games!

Here's a tip to end the blame game quickly: say "I'm sorry this happened. How can we fix it?"

Fighting Dirty

Hitting below the belt, public humiliation, throwing old mud in a new disagreement, bringing other people into the conflict (particularly hypothetical people, people you once knew). These are just a few examples of dirty fighting. Granted, it can be *very* difficult to fight fair, because there are usually several different emotions at play. Anything from frustration and annoyance to resentment and distrust. Nevertheless, it's very important to fight fair! Both sides usually feel heard and its an assertive communication, not aggressive!

First, instead of calling it fighting, call it an *argument*. Fighting has violent connotations with a lot of anger attached. This puts both partners on the defensive, and it's hard to get your point across, let alone settled. It's easier to argue and end with, "Let's agree to disagree...." My husband and I say that a lot! Disagreements are a kinder way to carry on communication, without the negative connotations of the word *fight*. You want to put your point of view forward, not club them with it; you want to be assertive, not aggressive!

Timing is very important when fighting fair. If you start an argument just as your partner is walking in the door from work, that would be fighting unfairly, like an ambush. You also don't want to start a conversation about your relationship if your partner is upset about something else—that's like kicking them when they're down. Plus, they are more than likely going to transfer that unrelated incident to the one you are trying to discuss—you want a clean slate when you put your cards on the table, not a surface covered with other issues.

If you are upset about something not related to your relationship, then let your partner know, "I just need to vent," and then vent. This way, your partner won't feel like you are attacking them. It also lets them know right off the bat your upset is not about them, but about a situation. It helps them keep their guard down so they can listen without pressure of having to solve something.

To *fight fair*, pick a time to vent or bring up an annoyance that is good for *both* of you. Don't do it during the big game; it will only be a source of aggravation—for both of you. Choose a time when your partner also hasn't had a bad day at work or is tired from a long day and already frustrated.

It's always good to start with something like "I had a bad day and need to vent; can I vent to you?" A good partner (if you chose a time they weren't busy) will most likely put down what they are doing and sit while you vent. The way you say things is more important that what you say! This will require a lot of practice. Just start by thinking about why you are frustrated, upset, emotional, hurt, etc., before talking.

Counselors have suggested this method to me, and it works, so I'm passing it on to you: Learn different words for how you feel. Remember to be specific. It's much less confrontational if you start with "*I feel* ..." Some examples are" I feel hurt; I feel embarrassed; I feel stupid when you say ...; I feel bad when ...; I feel like you don't respect my opinion ...; and so on. Put some thought into that sentence. It might help you stay more in charge of your emotions and clear in your mind during an argument.

I have also found it easier if you can back up your feelings with concrete examples. Your feelings can't be wrong, if that's how you honestly feel. I realize this makes the argument premeditated, but those may be the best kind. You know what you want to say and how you feel and can maybe get your point across better if you don't get too distraught or wound up.

Always try to end your argument on a positive note. You may say, "Thanks for being fair, thanks for listening," or something humorous like, "You still drive me crazy, but I love that it's still *you* that's driving me!" Ending with a positive statement about your partner is always helpful!

To fight fair you should avoid never and always. This will immediately be a lose-lose conversation and put your partner on the defensive. No one can *always* do something or *never* do something in a relationship! These words only show anger or resentment, not fairness and respect. Be honest without being cruel or condescending. Try to say what you mean without adding hurtful words. Most of the time you don't need to be blunt to get your honest point across.

I do realize how difficult this is! Emotions make people say and do things they may not mean to say. If you both realize this, then be honest after the tempers calm down and go back to each other and apologize for the hurtful comments. Saying "I'm sorry" is very important in a relationship.

Remember to thank your partner for what they do, even if you feel it should be expected (replacing toilet paper, picking up socks, etc.). It really can turn a bad situation or argument into pleasant, more open communication. Who doesn't enjoy positive, rewarding or comforting words!

Chapter II
Questions to Ask Yourself before Marriage

When deciding whether or not couples want to go further in their relationship and get engaged, people usually question if they are doing the right thing. That is normal because commitment is deep; it's serious; it's important. When you step back and question yourself, it is also good because it implies you are thinking. It's the work ahead that is the hard part.

Do I think with my head or my heart?

This chapter will offer ideas to help you answer that question. You have already thought with your heart when you met your partner. Now I believe you should think with your head. Your logical side will make you able to make better decisions in your relationship.

When you think with your heart, I call that the honeymoon period. Everything is wonderful and you let behaviors and annoyances go. You should not allow that because if you aren't honest from the first day, when the honeymoon period is over, your partner may become confused about who you really are.

Why do we choose the partner we do?

Every person brings *baggage* into the relationship. This means that whatever your past experiences, good or bad, will carry over to your relationship. What is your family background? Were the significant adults in your life happy, well adjusted, encouraging, supportive? Were they alcoholics, absent, unsupportive, verbally harsh, or abusive? These different backgrounds may determine who you choose as a partner.

Psychologists have postulated that you look for someone like your mother or father to marry because they were your first relationship. It is what and who you are comfortable with. After all, your partner would then *feel* like family.

People, in general, are very uncomfortable with change, new experiences, jobs, etc. This can lead to choosing a good or bad partner depending on your upbringing. This is why history can repeat itself, but it can also be a great time to break bad cycles and make better choices.

Let's start with the positive background! If your parents—or at least one parent—was supportive of your aspirations and goals, you may be more willing to adventure out and try new things. If your parents or other family members have shown you how to succeed in a relationship by showing you how to communicate, settle disagreements, etc., you will likely carry that into your relationship. If you come from parents who knew how to make a functional environment of love and respect, you were likely able to recognize what type of person you want to be and find in a life partner. You were fortunate to see what it took to be in a healthy relationship and the work involved. Your folks were not only supportive of you, but they also set a standard for you of acceptable behaviors, morality, and self-esteem. These are all healthy qualities to have when choosing a partner.

If you didn't grow up with happy, healthy adult models for choosing a partner, you will need to be more aware of what qualities you *want* in a partner, because it won't be instinctive. It can be more difficult when you've had a difficult past. You might have learned what you didn't like about your parents' relationship and will look for someone with opposite characteristics. Parents can be a good model for what *not* to do when choosing a partner also!

As a teacher of young adults, I have watched abused children grow up to be abusive adults. It's sad to see, but that is the way they have learned to solve problems. I have studied why children grow into abusive partners or look for abusive partners. Children learn by example.

As a child, you became familiar or comfortable with negative feelings and may not have even realized that there are happy feelings too. If you are told for sixteen years how bad you are at something, you start believing it. I spent a lot of years trying to show my students that good feelings are great to have. They still felt more comfortable with negative feelings. It took an average of one to three years for them to even start to consider they were worth feeling good about themselves. They had no hope of getting out of the cycle or understanding that it's *not* okay to abuse others or be abused. I spent every year teaching these young adults life skills, how people should be treated, and building their self-esteem so they might realize they are worth more than their parents made them believe they were worth.

If this describes you or someone you know, it can take years and a lot of professional counseling to break the cycle. I am hoping that if you are one of these people, you will not pick the same kind of partner. *You can break the cycle* by speaking to someone! Expect it to take a while but it can be done!

Can we break the cycle?

There are ways to break the cycle for those with difficult childhoods. There is a great deal of information out there that will help you dig deeper into your personal story. It requires more in-depth work, but the work may help you down the road when you are ready to find a partner that can make life more complete and healthy.

Getting an education is key in stepping ahead! If you are thinking about getting married and don't have a high school diploma, set the goal that you won't get married until you have your GED.

When you feel ready or are tired of struggling, think about getting a college education. It can be a trade school, business school, associate's degree, or bachelor's degree. Whatever your interests and financial situation allows. It will open up a lot of doors for you to meet new people who share your desire for higher education. You should also experience more confidence and self-worth, which is helpful in choosing a life partner. People who choose to go back to college are also older and not so persuaded by peer pressure—you never know, you might enjoy education now. You have matured and realize the importance of an education!

An example of this was my niece (on my husband's side), who came from an alcoholic, abusive background. When I met her, she had the same life she'd grown up with. She married an alcoholic who wasn't very nice, though not physically abusive. As she matured and spent more time with my husband and me, she saw a different life was possible, and we spent a lot of time encouraging her to shoot for the life she wanted and could have. She realized she wanted a better life for her and her three girls.

My husband and I encouraged her to go back to school at age twenty-six. She kept coming up with excuses why she couldn't: she had three children ranging in age from ten to three; she worked part time, was too old, couldn't afford it, and so on. I finally talked her into it after a few months, and her husband said he would help with the kids so she could go back to school. She got financial aid, and she knew that if my husband and I could help, we would be there for her. She didn't live close enough for me to pop by and baby-sit (about forty minutes away), but she stopped at our house on nights she had classes (we lived close to the college).

She would tell us about school, problems and struggles she was facing. We listened and kept encouraging her, especially because it was so difficult for her. We would sometimes take the kids on a weekend, if her husband couldn't, so she could study. We also helped her out with book purchases or anything else we could.

I watched the wonderful transformation of a young woman with no hope of a better life to someone having hope and a pathway to a better life. She no longer felt she had to repeat her mother's mistakes. She became a better mother, more positive, and more filled with happiness. It definitely helps to have a support system!

She saw the advantages of going to school, loved college, and met lots of new people—some who shared her experiences with life and others who had it easier. It opened up her eyes to new possibilities, and she graduated with a 3.8 grade point average. She felt great about her accomplishment and was a great example to her children.

She got a good paying job right away as a nurse, and a year later realized that she didn't want to be married to an alcoholic. She, as well as her children, raised their self-esteem and she felt she could do anything she set her mind to. The children were so proud of their mother's accomplishment and hard work that their self-esteem was raised by proxy.

It was very difficult and stressful to accomplish what she did, but she says now that it's over that it was all worth it. She has since divorced her husband and is meeting people who are intelligent, kind, and make a good living. Her children are also planning on going to college because of the example of success set by their mother!

The cycle was broken with her and for her kids. Her ex-husband, sadly did not take the steps necessary for him and is still in the cycle. But she no longer allows anyone to treat her with disrespect! Sadly, she has lost some friends and some family relationships because of her changes. Be aware, if you find the courage to break the cycle, this may happen. Misery loves company, and my niece and her children are no longer miserable. Those who still are seem to fear that she thinks she is too good for them. It's possible that she is.

If you share this experience or know someone like this, truck loads of encouragement needs to be available. If you don't know someone who could support you, call a teacher you built a relationship with and ask them for help. As a retired teacher, I use to love when my students would visit and let me know how they were doing. I was also always willing to help them any way I could. I believe most teachers share that compassion.

The second way to break the cycle is through *counseling!*. This way may take longer than college, but it certainly requires the same hard work. You have to be honest with a good counselor after you find one you trust. When selecting a social worker or counselor, keep in mind that they are not there to placate you or make you feel better about who you are now, but about who you can become. A good counselor (and I know this from many years of experience) will not always agree with you, but challenge you to find different and healthier ways to look at things. They can support you emotionally while you break the cycle.

Chapter 12
Red Flags

A red flag is a warning that tells you trouble could be brewing if you don't fix the situation. It refers to small things you notice that will likely lead to bigger issues. Issues between you that come up while you're dating will be bigger issues once you live together or get married. That's where your potential partner's issues (referred to previously as *baggage*) could carry over into the relationship, or where your *respective* baggage might interact in dangerous ways. These might be unrealistic expectations, points of contention, or dysfunctional reactions, but whatever they are, they need to be addressed before marriage! All relationships come with some type of baggage—expect that—but some of the baggage, like the ones listed below, can cause more stress than you may be able to handle.

Here are some examples of red flags you definitely should not ignore. Make sure you address them early in the relationship! Have clear guidelines for what is *expected* of you and your partner.

Using texting as a substantial form of communication

Are you or your partner always texting each other, even when you are in the same area, (house, store, etc.)? I love my cell phone and it's great for messages, business calls, but never for conversations with my partner. I find too many couples using cell phones as a way to communicate emotional issues in a relationship. It has developed into an easy—shall I say *lazy?*—way to communicate, without intonation or feelings for both partners. I call this a red flag because replacing personal communication with cell phones can be dangerous to your relationship. Arguments, feelings, and problems can't be deciphered in text. You have to hear and see the body language to understand the complete intent of your partner. I know of couples who have broken up over a text that was misinterpreted because they couldn't hear the intonation in their partner's voice.

Intonation, or the way things are said, are sometimes more important than what is said. Let me give you a clear example. Your partner can say "yes, dear" in very different ways: sarcastic, friendly, or loving. You can't tell which they intend in a text, because you can't read the intonation. You have to hear it! Can you read if someone is sad, upset, or frustrated with a text? No. Unless they text that they are upset, you won't know. Even if they do text that they are upset, will you know to what degree they are upset?. I truly believe that texting should only be used for minor, factual messages.

My son learned this the hard way when his live-in girlfriend texted him about a really bad day she was having. Since he couldn't hear in her voice how upset she was, he just texted back that he was sorry she'd had a bad day and then wrote "What do you want to do tonight?" When she got home, she was very upset with *him*. She felt he didn't care about her, and he felt ambushed because he couldn't understand why she was so upset. They argued about his perceived lack of concern, which led to more arguing. It became a larger issue for her, and shortly after that things fell apart and they broke up. It was all miscommunication, because she texted something that should have been said in person. If he could've read her body language and heard her tone, he would have responded differently.

Texting is great for short, declarative messages: *I'm on my way home … Meet me at 8. Can't w8 to c u….* A friend of mine said his wife goes to bed while he watches TV in the other room. She will text him if the TV is too loud. I thought it was great. She sent a message quietly so as not to wake the children, and she didn't have to get out of bed to tell him. Texting to say I love you, have a good day, pick up bread, etc.—those messages are what technology, in my opinion, is good for. They help make our lives convenient.

Using technology to avoid participating in your relationship

Playing video games is an example of this. I have been to several homes over the past twenty years where the teenagers and twenty-something's are playing video games. They don't develop good social skills that way!

They don't say hello, stop or pause the game to have a conversation with flesh-and-blood human beings. Their digital interactions are more important than their human interactions. Does this sound like your partner? Could you say the house is burning and they'd respond with, "Okay honey, I'll be their soon!" *They aren't listening.* This is a huge red flag!

If your partner is one of these people, you will need to discuss this and be *very* clear that you need to set concrete limitations to the time allotted for game playing.

If your partner is thirty years or older and is still behaving like a teenager with the game playing, you need to take a very serious look at whether or not this is a life-partner you can count on to be a mature, reliable partner! How they spend their own time is one thing, but how they spend *together time* is something else altogether. What are you looking for in a companion? Is this a person who can look up from their video game or other private playtime activity to be a partner to you? Or are they going to put your relationship into a more parent/child role? It may sound harsh, but consider moving on now if you are wondering these things yourself. They may not be able to fill your need for security, belongingness, and love.

If you are using technology, particularly the internet, for entertainment other than games, you will find fantasy and temptation that are detrimental in a marriage. I have seen this so many times. If you are using it for meeting people of the opposite sex, you will have a problem. It's an easy way to carry on unhealthy fantasies. Do you really know who you are talking to? No! Are you trying to get validation for your feelings because you are insecure in your real relationship? It won't help.

When it comes to meeting people on the internet, you have to be able to separate fantasy from reality. That can be very hard to do because most people want fantasy. Cheating on the internet is a worldwide problem. Dr. Phil defined cheating as "anything you would not do in front of your partner." I couldn't agree more! How would you feel if your partner was cheating on you? You are probably thinking, *it would be over!* Then why would you do something to your partner that you wouldn't want done to you?

If you want to chat on the internet, include your partner in the conversations or, at the very least, let them know you are chatting and let them read the conversations. If your partner is not comfortable with your conversations, then you will have to talk about limits and guidelines for them and keep them transparent or share them with your partner. You must be able to trust each other.

Drinking, and Drinking and Driving

I'm not referring to social drinking. I'm referring to drinking that interferes with your relationship. That shows disrespect to your very being. Almost everyone enjoys a drink or two at parties or when they go out. If your partner doesn't embarrass you by the amount they drink, you shouldn't have a problem with drinking. If one of you agrees to be the designated driver, you are on the right track.

But if it is a concern, ask yourself these questions: Does your partner like to drink at parties and you don't? Are you *always* the designated driver? When your partner drinks, does he/she embarrass you? Do they get behind the wheel no matter who else is in the car? These would definitely need to be resolved before the marriage.

You should come to some kind of compromise about how much they drink before it is out of hand and who is going to drive. My ex-husband use to enjoy more drinks than I was comfortable with, and drive home, even when the kids were in the car. Back then, we didn't have police checkpoints, so he didn't consider it an issue. Before we went out though, I would tell him I wanted the keys to drive home. He disagreed and would drive home. We couldn't resolve the issue by that time. That's why you need to have these conversations before you marry.

Remember, marriage is about teamwork and fairness. If neither of you can remember who was the DD last, then mark it down on your calendar. Or take a cab to and from the party. These solutions will help avoid an argument, and possibly save someone's life.

Flirting

Flirting *can* also be another big red flag. The definition for flirting in the context of relationships is anything that makes your partner uncomfortable, even suspicious of your intentions with the *flirted*. If your partner is a flirt, and you don't like it, you need to tell them. Their response may also show a lack of respect for your feelings. Be clear about what you mean by flirting! There is genuine flirting and there is needless jealousy, which is another red flag altogether. So be sure to define it clearly.

If flirting is excessive, you or partner may consider it cheating, which, again, see Dr. Phil's definition, Would you act like that if your partner was next to you? Make sure you and your partner can agree on a definition so there is no misunderstanding down the road of whether there was cheating or uncomfortable flirting. If it offends your partner, respect their feelings enough to tone down your flirting to something acceptable to both of you. You can tone it down by using less physical contact like hugging or touching the entire time you are talking to the recipient of the flirting. If you tone it down to just talking to a friend but your partner is still upset you are talking to the opposite sex, that's a real sense of insecurity that would also need to be dealt with.

If you flirt with someone to the point *they* think you are single, you have crossed the line! If you joke or spend all your time with a sexually or romantically available person for too long and don't include your partner in any of these conversations, that may be hurtful to your partner. If it is, then include your partner in those conversations; that way, they know what you are talking about and there is no threat involved. If your partner is sensitive to these situations, and I feel they should be, then you need to make them feel more secure and respected.

One way to do this is by complimenting your partner in front of your friends or bragging about their accomplishment on how well they put the party together, their job, or whatever is appropriate. This goes a long way in relieving stress for your partner.

If you are both flirtatious with others, you might want to rethink if you are ready to settle down with each other. It may seem like a small issue you can solve now, but think long term. Do you both enjoy flirting with the opposite sex, and it doesn't bother your partner? This would go against human nature and the need for belongingness. At some point, one or both partners could go too far with the flirting, and one will get hurt. I believe it also shows a great lack of respect for your partner.

My son's friend is an example of flirtations gone awry. He was always known as a *player*. He called it "harmless flirtation." He liked to e-mail old girlfriends, meet a nice-looking woman and send her text messages or e-mails. When he married his "dream girl", we all thought those flirtatious ways had stopped. Less than a year later, she caught him e-mailing other women. Had he been upfront and done his e-mailing in front of her, she might not have taken it as a threat. She walked out on him that week; it was hands-down unacceptable behavior to her. He was crushed. Could they have discussed whether such behavior was cheating as she considered it or just maintaining friendships as he claimed? Could they have discussed it and resolved it *before* marriage? I'm guessing he was hiding it from her on purpose, hoping to never get caught—either he knew how she would take it, or he had not given up his player ways. The marriage was over that fast.

Remember the core of a personality doesn't change; it can usually only be modified. But *if* you are open and honest you can work through most issues.

Obsessions

Obsessive behaviors can be another red flag. Is one partner spending more time with their obsession then they are with you? That's when one partner spends an unreasonable amount of time with their obsession and it interferes with your time together. It can range from something small like obsessing over a television show to buying real estate.

How much time does your partner spend watching sports, reality shows, soap operas, reading books (except this one!), playing games, shopping? If your partner does display an obsessive behavior, does it interfere with your relationship? If it does not interfere with the relationship, it isn't a red flag. Make sure you think long term here! Is their potential for it to turn into a red flag?

I have a nephew who is in a serious relationship. He would watch nothing but sports all day and night before the relationship. She is watching sports with him now, but does she really want to in the long term? Does your partner spend more time away from you than with you (men or women)? Acknowledging this obsession before marriage can help you discuss compromises and limitations before you're up to your eyeballs in alone time. Make sure you are honest about this—with yourself and your partner.

If they have respect for you and your feelings, a compromise should be obtainable. Whether it's shopping, money, or sports, compromise—be clear, set limits, and agree to comply. Practice this agreement before you walk down the aisle. This will also give you an idea of how sincere your partner is on making the marriage work. How much effort are they really willing to put into making the marriage a success?

Intrusive parents, family members, friends

These can cause a red flag if your partner's parents or friends—or your parents and friends—can't respect your—or your partner's—wishes on boundaries, rules, limits, etc. If they want to control the aspects of your or your partner's life that they did before you were together, there can be trouble. Watch closely how each of you responds to these old relationships when they interfere with yours. It's usually a need for control on the part of the in-laws or the old gang, and a test for which relationship is going to take primacy.

I have a sister who experienced this in an early relationship with the father of her son. Her partner's mother was so domineering over him that when my sister came along, she wanted to dominate her as well. She dated him for a long time hoping he would change but the apron strings were too strong. She realized she couldn't deal with her future mother-in-law's lack of respect for her and the boundaries she tried to set. Her partner was not willing to go along with my sister or back her up for fear of alienating his mother. It ended with my sister and her son's father breaking up.

Does your partner make decisions based around their family or friends and not want to deal with yours? Are the parents supportive with your decisions (and your partners) or do they try to sway you to choose what they think is best? This can be as simple as ordering from a menu to what kind of house you should buy. Be aware of that and discuss limits of parental/family/friends involvement in your personal lives. Then be aware if your partner abides by the agreement. This red flag needs to be obliterated before marriage.

This will be very important when you start having children or if one of you has an opportunity that might take you both out of town. How much do they try to turn it into their experience rather than celebrating yours?

Another clue to this red flag would be how much your partner needs to call their parents. Do they have to call for parental approval or advice to make a significant purchase? Do they confide in their parents more than they do you? Do they feel more comfortable inviting parents to all your social events even if it's not a parental type party (beer blast)?

A good rule to set down from the beginning or if considering children is placing a limit on family/friend involvement. You might have to be clear that they must call the day *before* they want to stop by. They can only come over a certain number of days a week, whatever is appropriate for your situation. Make sure you come up with a plan that you can *both* agree to! And then really work to stick to the guidelines you have set! If the partner can't agree to reasonable terms, you may want to rethink your relationship—or get outside help if their other qualities are just too good to throw away.

Not being able to admit when you are wrong

Do they seem to know everything or have an answer for everything? Do they feel it's a weakness to be wrong? Do you? This can be a huge red flag. This usually stems from insecurity. This is a tough one to change or even modify, especially if they are above the normal range of competitive. This tendency needs to be handled gently—if not professionally. The insecurity usually stems from unresolved issues in childhood. The only way to deal with this, in my experience, is to use positive reinforcement or physical proof they are incorrect. Don't use the word *wrong*. Incorrect or misinformed is a much nicer way of saying they were wrong.

Choose your battles. Is this one worth ruining your evening? Would you rather be right or happy? When my husband is convinced he is right, and I can prove he isn't, I will show him the evidence that points to where he is misinformed (avoid *wrong*). If it's something I can't prove is right but *feel* I am, I ask myself, *How important is it to be right?* I'd rather be happy! His need to be right also stems from his childhood, and I am aware of that so I can usually—not always, but usually—accept that personality glitch.

Counseling may be the best option if this red flag is familiar to you.

Spending and Debts

Does your potential partner spend more money than they make and think nothing about it because they will pay it off with their bonus, raise, or credit card? Make sure you are honest about this, with yourself and your partner. What do you do if the situation changes? It's better to live *below* your means than at or above them. Remember, you can't predict the future. If your partner does spend too freely, discuss this prior to marriage. Maybe you can both sit down and restate your goals. How much money would you both need to save to buy a house, take a vacation, etc.? If your partner over-spends (women call it *retail therapy!*), make sure they are invested in the discussion and can agree to a realistic budget you can both afford.

Bridezilla!

Planning for the wedding can become a red flag. Of course I understand the importance of this special day. A lot of women who want a large wedding actually put their relationship on hold to focus their attention on the spectacle of a perfect wedding day. *Big mistake!* Think about this! Your wedding takes months to plan and a lot of hard work, and for what? Your ONE *special day.*

How realistic is it that you stop working on your relationship in order to insure one nice day? Keep your wedding in perspective to the larger picture. Apply all that effort to your relationship, which you want to last a lifetime instead of the one day you wear your dream dress (that maybe you can't afford) in order to have that "perfect" wedding. Wouldn't you rather have the perfect marriage?

Talk to your partner, try to involve them. If they don't want to get involved—for whatever reason—then talk about hiring a wedding planner. If you can't afford one, then you get some close friends involved and have your partner go with you. The wedding ceremony is the event that cements your vows, the way you see yourself as a couple, and how you want to present yourselves to your family, friends, and whatever higher authority you have chosen to declare yourselves before (church, creator, nature, city hall, etc.). Both of you should be involved in putting it together. If nothing else, at least you will both see where the money is going and one of you can try to be *the voice of reason* in the spending. Remember that if you put the time into your relationship like you do your wedding, you may actually get the fairy tale. Remember, you don't find true love, you make it happen.

Absentee Partner

Do you or your partner spend too much time watching sports or shopping or partying with old friends but not with you? If you are okay with this now, think long term. Spending too much time apart can be a problem. It doesn't make for a secure feeling about how much you love or care for each other if you don't spend some of your free time together.

Will it still be okay to go off separately when you have children? Why wouldn't your partner invite you? Do you trust they are where they say they are? It's very important to discuss this. A few couples I interviewed included one partner who did this kind of thing. The wife thought it was okay until the situation changed. Children came along and, now a young mother, she wanted more help. This one particular partner didn't want to change and didn't see why he should, since it had been allowed pre-children. It then became a problem resolving his "party ways" post children. Make sure your partner wants to participate and not just be there when it's convenient for them!

If your partner prefers to spend time without you and makes you feel unimportant or not relevant in the relationship, don't guess why, ask them! Do not accept "I don't know" for an answer! You need to be honest and tell your partner that it bothers you and you want to be included in their plans. This applies to both sexes! If they are not willing, you may want to walk away because it will get worse once you get married! Most people think things get better and the bad behaviors will diminish. That is one of those fantasies, remember!

Attached at the Hip

On the other hand, if your partner wants to spend all their time with you and avoids longtime friendships because you are now their life, this may be also be red flag. Ask your partner why they don't hang out with their old friends. Maybe you could set something up where you all go out together with your partner's friends.

It's always a good idea to maintain friendships that you have had. It can help you incorporate those previous good memories into your new memories. For most people, there is comfort in those friends; they probably know you pretty well and may be able to give you and your partner insights into your relationship. It's fun to hear the old stories of when your partner was a teen (if you didn't know each other then).

***

There will be many little things in your marriage that might annoy you about your partner. Expect it! In the larger picture, do you really want to argue over picking up your socks, or other insignificant issues? Choose the battles that are really important and make those work! The important ones were the ones you already read : finances, children, what personalities may go well with yours.

Whether it's shopping, money, sports, etc., you will need to compromise, set limits, be clear, and agree to it. Practice this agreement process together before you walk down the aisle. This will also give you an idea of how sincere your partner is about making the marriage work. How much effort are you both really willing to put into making the marriage a success?

Saying that, if you are looking for a happy partnership, then I don't believe any of the red flags are okay to live with. They may vary in degree of seriousness, but the applicable ones should be dealt with. Don't take any of these issues for granted. During my interviews, couples with two or more of these issues admitted they had problems in their marriage. If something works for one of you or both of you, just make sure you discuss it, why it's okay or not okay, and what happens when the situation changes.

Are you both willing to change or does one of you believe *take me as I am*? Life will change you, believe me. Are you both flexible and willing to change for the benefit of the relationship? Do you believe changing will help your relationship? It might be easier to just find someone else! This is another reason communication, mutual respect, and being considerate of your partner (as well as others) is so important. Keep those lines of communication open, so as each of you changes, you can change together.

If you find that several of these red flags are displayed in your relationship, you may want to reconsider if they are the right partner for you! It's okay to realize it now before you pay a large amount of money for a wedding or waste *good years* trying to change your partner.

A counselor once told me that I would be happier alone and not so stressed than to be in a bad marriage. He was right! Once I divorced, I had the energy to enjoy my children, friends and family more, instead of stressing over what argument I was going to face that day. Sidebar: my ex-husband and I are still friends and attend parties together when our children are involved.

Remember, *a long-term relationship is priceless; divorce isn't. I know I am repeating myself but that's how important the message is.*

Summary

Here are some topics that I hope you remember and apply to your daily life. You and your partner should have ideas about what to expect and a plan to make it happen the way you want it to. These were the top compatibility issues based on my survey with happily married couples:

- Don't think of yourself as married but living with a great teammate. Encourage them when they aren't doing well and cheer for them when they are! Remember, you really are on the same team!
- Your partner can't read your mind. If you want something be clear, pick a good time when your partner isn't busy or stressed and tell them what you want. *Explain* how you are feeling as clearly as you can.
- Use good manners. I can't stress enough how *please, thank-you* and *sorry* can change your partner's (and your) mood immediately. It's also helpful if you ask your partner to help with something instead of telling them. Make sure you thank them!
- Treat your partner like you would a friend. Ask yourself, *is this how I would treat a friend*? If it's not, change it! Your partner may not feel like your best friend now, but hopefully over the years, they will grow to be.
- Sex fades, sometimes becomes extinct (guys, stop freaking out on this one), but can increase your level of *intimacy* (a feeling of closeness that comes from knowing a person so well you are in sync). It's a deeper connection than anything you can imagine today. Hopefully, you will become your partner's best friend *with benefits!*
- Understand that the person you marry today will not be the same person five, ten, twenty years from now. They may still be the

same *core* person (optimistic, selfish, kind, happy, shy, etc.), but on the level, evolution dictates that people will change. This has to occur for several reasons. It may be a job, children, moving, physical illness, emotional maturity, chronological maturity. Were you the same person you were in high school, college?

- How does your partner relate to his or her parents? Does the son have respect for his mother, or not? Does she dote on him? If he does(respect) and she doesn't (dote), he will probably have respect for you. How does he get along with his father? If he has him in a good perspective, it will tell you what kind of father he will be. Does the daughter have a sweet relationship with her father or troubled? Does she see her mother as a human being in her own right, or are they at each other's throats? These relationships will give you some indication of how she might treat you and your children.

- Make sure you have similar goals. Do you both believe your children, if you have them, should go to college, work for what they want, or do you believe in spoiling them? Do you believe in corporal discipline, grounding children, or letting them choose their own punishment? What form of correction do you both want to use? Positive reinforcement works better than negative reinforcement.

- Are you both free or tight with money? Remember to follow your plan for finances. Modifying it as your marriage changes.

- Are you both outgoing or homebodies or one of each?

- It's helpful if you have some interests in common. Do you both like to socialize, have parties, enjoy entertaining, enjoy staying home, enjoy participating in sports or watching them, etc.?

- Maintain the little things—even if it's hard, as it will be at times—kiss your partner goodbye, hello, say I love you before you go to sleep, be courteous and thoughtful to one another and gracious when receiving courtesies (opening doors, bringing a cup of coffee, etc.).

- Do you see counseling as an avenue to strengthen your bond or an admission of weakness and failure to be avoided? If you are having trouble, can you both agree that this would be a good avenue to explore before the relationship becomes to frustrating? Outsiders are not personally invested and can be more objective..

- Remember the bad times will pass if you address the issues that come up with the techniques you have learned here. The reward for doing a good job will come—the pride you feel when you can both walk *your* children down the aisle, confident they have chosen well; the togetherness of babysitting the grandchildren; and the enjoyment of the retirement you both planned when you were young.

- It really is very rewarding when you learn to make it through life together, and it may be a lot healthier for your children to learn that parents can argue and struggle in their marriage but find a way to work through it.

- Start disagreements with "I feel" and finish arguments with a positive comment about your partner, or at least a kiss.

- Give your partner space. Spend time developing your own hobbies and interests.

- Sense of humor is very important in relieving stress in a marriage. Don't take things too seriously. *Sarcasm* is not a good type of humor. It is mean humor!

- Good communication skills are vital in a long-term, successful relationship. By now, I hope I have stressed the importance of this idea. There should be no judging your partner ("that was stupid," or eye rolling, etc.) when you are arguing. They are just telling you how they feel, whether you agree or not. *Respect* what your partner has to say, whether you agree or not.

- *Accept* your partner for who they are. No one is perfect, and you have flaws that your partner has to accept too.

- *It's a job **and** an adventure.* Understand that if you treat your marriage like a job, it means you show up every day, take responsibility for your part, and get better at it as you gain more experience.

- Finally, it is important to stay flexible and compromise! There will be fun parts, exciting parts, boring parts, and parts that make you say, "What was I thinking?" Stay flexible to the changes and maintain a sense of humor!

Work hard, stay focused, and the rewards are priceless.

Appendix
Interviews with Couples Who Have Been Married More Than 20 Years.

This section reveals how couples married more than twenty years did on the survey you took at the beginning of the book. They were asked some of the same questions and other relevant questions for their age. I did not ask them, for example, if they *want* children but if they *had* children. I spoke with couples at various levels of education, socioeconomic status, and marriages that ranged from twenty-one years up to thirty-six years.

These interviews were also done in-person. I sat with each couple and asked them to do the survey together. I gave them each an answer sheet with their partner's name at the top and asked them to answer as if *they were their partner*. When the questions were answered, I would give the answer sheet back to the other partner and ask the same questions again. This time, each partner would answer about themselves. This way the couple could compare their partner's answers to their own answer of how they saw themselves.

They then had to answer a few questions independently. All the couples enjoyed finding out what their partner thought vs. what they thought, after so many years together.

You might draw comparisons from your relationship when you see how they resolved similar issues. Compare what you consider the important issues in your relationship to theirs. You can see how they made it work, why it worked, take away some useful tips. The important lesson to take away from the reading is *how* they made it work and what traits they have in common and which are different. No one is always happy, but pay attention to how much time these couples spent arguing and resolving their issues and try to focus on that in your relationship. Some names have been changed.

Chuck and Maria

This couple has been married for thirty-one years as of 2012. I have known them for roughly ten years and have always admired their relationship. Chuck is a semi-retired electrical engineer at a large company, and Maria works out of her house as an esthetician, performing facials and other skin-care treatments. They are empty-nesters and grandparents.

Maria is mildly pessimistic while Chuck is a moderate optimist. They felt that these differences played off each other well.

When they got to question 30 (Do you text your partner more than you talk?), they both had a lot to say! Chuck is very comfortable with technology, since he uses it daily in his job. Maria has an iPad and uses it often. Both stated that when they go out to restaurants or movies, they have witnessed young couples sitting across from each other, never talking or even making eye contact: they are too busy with their phones! This drives Chuck and Maria crazy, they told me, because they know how important communication is in a healthy marriage and how few young people seem to understand how important actual talking is.

Chuck commented during the interview process that "I feel personal contact is *very* important, and technology is driving people away from that."

Maria noted how bothered she was that one couple they watched over the course of their entire meal, never once made eye contact with each other because they were so busy with their phones. Maria also was very bothered that the two didn't even talk.

Chuck said that he would like to see technology used only for what it was intended. "Don't use it to avoid your partner."

Here was their idea or example of using technology appropriately: They love to sit together sometimes and play Scrabble. They use their iPad because the computer keeps the score. It's convenient and allows them time to discuss words, more time to talk and drink wine!

The final question was "How do you rate your marriage?"

Both said "Very happy."

I asked them to share something about their marriage early on. I asked about things that aggravated them in the early parts of their marriage, vacations they took. They both looked at each other and remembered the same vacation and started to smile. At the time, they'd gotten aggravated with each other, it rained, meals didn't always go well. Today, those memories made them smile.

I asked them how long they remember staying mad at each other. The both said, simultaneously, that it was "never more than a week, two at the absolute worst." When I asked how they got over it, they also both agreed. They hated feeling unhappy for that length of time, so they would get together to talk about the problem and resolve it. They said, "We are both happy people, so feeling unhappy made us more miserable than what we were arguing about." They both agreed they would rather be happy than right. 96% of their answers matched after thirty-one years of marriage.

Mark and Mary

Mark and Mary have been married for twenty-four years. They got married when they were thirty years old, and Mark thought that attributed to the success in their marriage.

Mary has a master's degree, and Mark has an associate's degree. They have a daughter that is about to graduate college.

This couple answered twelve questions differently when they were answering for themselves and only eight when they answered for each other. I was surprised by these numbers, because I have known them for about thirty years, and I see how comfortable and happy they are with each other.

Mary and Mark agreed that Mary was a highly emotional women with little patience, but nevertheless an optimist. They also agreed that Mark was a pessimist, though patient and moderately emotional. This is an example of how opposites can attract and work through problems together.

In addition, Mark gives Mary control of the relationship to avoid conflict. It works for them. This may be another reason their marriage has worked for so long. He also stated that he would rather be happy, while Mary stated she would rather be right ... because that makes her happy! Mark admitted he is laid back and very uncomfortable with conflict. He believes that it's not worth the arguing, and stated that Mary usually *was* right, because she thinks things through. Mark admitted that he just says the first thing he is thinking, without really thinking things through, adding, "That's why my wife is always right."

They are from similar socioeconomic backgrounds. They both came from middle class families. Mary said her family was more dysfunctional than Mark's. Her parents argued often and did not spend time together. She said that she grew up in a household where parents didn't divorce, happy or not. Mark said he thought his parents were happy.

They also believe that there needs to be time spent with just the two of them whether it's a date night or just hanging out when they are home alone. They both agreed that it's important to keep a date night. Mary said they never called it that, but they just enjoyed spending time together with each other.

Mark enjoys socializing more than Mary. She has no problem when he goes golfing or to Knights of Columbus to see his friends once a week or so. That's her time to read and relax on her own.

Mary makes the decisions when it comes to taking care of family, social events, planning for vacations. She has always been the strong one in the relationship and is comfortable in that role, because Mark "may not get it done," she said. He is comfortable with that assessment and the solution, and appreciates Mary's ability to handle the details.

In their marriage, Mary stated that she was mostly happy, and Mark stated he was very happy. Mary attributed their success in marriage because they were patient with each other. Mark attributed their success to enjoying each other's company and having his own time to go out with friends.

This couple complements each other's strengths and weaknesses. They have fun together! Mary runs the family, and Mark is happy letting her. Based on my knowledge, that could be why *she was only mostly happy,* and *he was very happy.* She carries the brunt of the work, feeling the need to hold the weight of the relationship, family, and social events. Over twenty-four years of marriage, they stated that only about two years, off-and-on, were rough. Those years were when their daughter was young.

Sharon and John

This couple has been married for twenty-one years. They have two children, both in college. They are a very busy couple, so getting them to sit down with me together was difficult.

When we started the survey, she was hesitant, because she didn't think she had the time. As the questions progressed, her hesitation lessened. She admitted she had a lot of fun learning her husband's answers and how it opened up dialog for both of them. They had very few differences in their perceptions about themselves and each other, but the ones they differed on surprised them.

Sharon is highly emotional and felt her husband was as well. John answered that Sharon was highly emotional and he was not. John also answered that Sharon would rather be right than happy, and she said she would rather be happy than right. Another question they didn't agree on was "Are you the life of the party or quiet?" Sharon felt they were both quiet, and John felt she was quiet but he was the life of the party ... after about an hour into the party.

When it came to the question of what do you do when the going gets tough, they also answered for each other differently. He said she would work through it while he would spend time alone thinking about the situation until he forgot what the situation was. So, I guess his answer was, when the going gets tough he forgets about it.

They both identified as optimistic people who spend a lot of time socializing with friends. They also agreed that they were both within the normal range of competitiveness. They agreed that it is was only in sports, and if they lost, they still enjoyed the party as much as the sport. When asked if they were competitive while arguing, they agreed they were not.

Like Mark in the couple above, John seems to be the one who enjoys going with the flow, because he would rather be happy than right.

He stated that he is uncomfortable with confrontation or arguing, so he tends to avoid it. He feels strongly about his family and money. When John discusses money, Sharon will back down if John loses his temper. They both stated their arguments are "always about something small and unimportant" but that they are" in sync" about everything major.

They don't stay mad at each other for more than a day, they said, because neither could remember what they were arguing about.

Sharon is the stronger one who, like Mary, does the planning for the family, vacations, and activities, children's schedules, events. She is a take-charge personality. John is usually agreeable to letting her take over those decisions.

Finally, John's answer to "What's the key to success?" was they have similar interests and are both fun-loving. Sharon's answer was they don't argue about anything but little things (they discussed all the big issues before they married, she said), they settle the argument with a kiss, and she tells him that he is the love of her life.

They scored a 93% on the compatibility survey.

Tom and Amanda

Tom and Amanda have been married for twenty-one years. They have two boys ages twelve and fourteen. Amanda has some higher education, while Tom has learned his trade through apprenticing.

They filled out the survey and there were several red flags. Both stated that they are not patient people. This leads to short tempers, and they admit it. Tom also stated that neither partner listens to the other. He stated that they don't get along well but are hanging in there because his "wife puts up with his crap."

He stated that he would rather be right than happy. Amanda would rather be happy. Tom sees no value in date night. When I asked him if he really felt that paying attention to his partner at least one night a week was important for the relationship, he said, no, I'm too busy with the boys.

Amanda, on the other hand, would like a date night and feels it might be helpful.

He also admitted that he is messy while Amanda prefers the home clean.

Tom thought he was an optimist, while Amanda thought he was a pessimist. She also stated she was a pessimist, and Tom agreed.

Out of thirty questions, ten were different. I could feel the tension during the interview. There appeared to be no respect for each other, and that is a huge red flag. They also had personality conflicts that could be considered red flags.

Neither partner was patient, and Tom saw no value in getting outside help to strengthen their marriage. Amanda feels counseling would be helpful, but they would both need to go in order to maximize the benefits. He is very competitive and would rather be right than happy. Since he is the stronger personality, this causes friction in arguments and leaves them unresolved. That has led to resentments, frustration, an inability to compromise, and at least one separation.

In the interview, I observed very little mutual respect for each other's opinions. Other couples I interviewed were able to laugh at the differences and talk about them; Tom and Amanda did not.

They also didn't agree on how to raise their boys. Amanda gives in to her children's wants, and Tom doesn't. There is a lack of mutual respect for how the other wants to correct their boys. Neither partner uses positive reinforcement, which adds to the tension in the entire family.

Tom and Amanda do have some similarities. They both enjoy socializing with friends, having parties and going to concerts. They also said they enjoy staying home at times. They both believe higher education is important for their boys. They do share the same goals for their boys, but don't seem to agree on how to make that happen. They will go to parent–teacher conferences together, but Tom said when the teacher gives them suggestions on how to help the boys, he doesn't agree and blames the teacher. Amanda will try to back up the teacher. I have met both boys, and they are very nice and polite, so they've done something right.

When they answered what is the key for your success, Tom wrote, "My wife puts up with my crap," and Amanda wrote, "It's best for the boys."

They disagreed on nine of the major questions. They are struggling in their marriage, but are still together. They scored a 70% on compatibility. They would probably benefit from marriage counseling, but Tom doesn't see value in that. They are staying together because, "It's easier to raise the boys with us together than apart."

The lesson I want to share from this interview is, that if you can stay together for twenty-one years, it is never too late to recognize your weaknesses and work on them, via professional help. Both partners *have to be willing* and open to it, however, and unfortunately one partner here is not. I wish them growth and success.

Laura and Bob

This couple has been married almost thirty-four years. They are in their early seventies and both act like they are in their forties. They are both very young at heart, think young, look young, and love to socialize. I mention this because when they told me their ages, I couldn't believe it. I have met seventy-year-olds that act and look eighty. I also thought that seventy was old, but not anymore!

This couple's answers agreed on all but two of the questions. When

Bob answered, "Would Laura rather be right than happy", he thought she needed to be right. Laura felt that she would rather be happy. When I asked her if she thought Bob was correct about her, she smiled and said that she was usually right and happy! They both smiled, and Bob said that's why he answered the way he did. She *likes* to be right.

The only other serious issue they didn't agree on was, "Does your partner listen to you?" Bob didn't feel that Laura listened to him, but she said Bob was a good listener and felt she was too. This is where Bob said that he doesn't let things like listening bother him, he just goes ahead with his day.

Both also agreed they were very happily married. Laura admitted there were difficult days when they were raising their children, but they never stayed angry or upset with each other for more than a day. They worked through it, discussed it, and compromised on a solution right away. Both again agreed they were happy people uncomfortable with … *unhappiness!*

What they did agree on that is very important in a good marriage was socializing together, having fun, and respecting one another. As much as they enjoy doing things together, they, like so many couples I interviewed, said they also have their own interests and their partner gives them the space to do their own thing.

They agreed they were both optimistic, generous with their money, but also able to save for things they want. They are also both compatible with regard to showing affection. Bob said Laura is very affectionate and he is sometimes affectionate; I consider that compatible, because they are not opposites.

Bob also has a good sense of humor and loves to be happy. Although Laura is more reserved, she too has a great sense of humor. This was shown in Bob's answer to, "What was the key to your success?" His answer was "good make-up sex!" Hers was more reserved. She wrote, "compromise, be considerate, make each other laugh and have fun." Both agreed they were very happily married. They had a 93% compatibility score.

Joe and Gregg

This couple has been together for twenty-one years. Joe is a nurse, while Gregg works for the postal service. Both enjoy socializing and quiet evenings at home. They were surprised during the survey at some of the answers each other gave, which opened up dialog between the two partners. They had a good time when I told them that it was good if one partner has to be right and the other would rather be happy, because it can be complementary.

Joe admitted that if it weren't for Gregg always taking charge of social functions like parties, vacations, and extreme couponing, the two of them couldn't do a lot of the things they enjoy together like vacationing and dining out with coupons. It drove Joe crazy that Gregg coupons everything, including restaurants, but admitted that if Gregg didn't take charge of that, they wouldn't be able to go out to dinner as often as they do. He realized that, even though it drives him crazy, he appreciated Greg's efforts where before the survey, he didn't.

They also admitted that they are both highly emotional, which could lead to arguments. Then they said they quickly realize how ridiculous the arguments are, and Gregg would be the one to back down, because he would rather be happy than right.

Joe admitted that money was very important to him, because he likes buying a car every year or two and loves real estate. Gregg stated that money is not that important to him but is very frugal. He doesn't understand Joe's passion for real estate and cars but doesn't get upset because he understands it's his partner's passion. He does however regulate his partner's passion by not letting Joe buy houses!

Both partners also agreed that they were good listeners and their communication was good. These qualities got them through difficult times in the relationship. When I asked them if they *hear* each other during an argument, they smiled at each other and said, "Eventually." They admitted that one may have to reiterate his point until the other understands it. They are both good at compromising in this situation.

They also agreed that Joe is the quiet one, and Gregg is the life of the party. This lets Joe off the hook for having to entertain, and he enjoys letting Gregg take over. Again, they are different here but in a complementary way.

The one issue for this couple was that Joe admitted he was pessimistic while Gregg was optimistic. This was okay for their situation because, according to Gregg, Joe is *mostly* pessimistic but can be an optimist about a few things. Gregg admitted that since he is an optimist, it "drives him crazy" that Joe can be very pessimistic about certain topics, but he understands that his partner is a pessimist, accepts it, and moves on.

Joe felt that with some issues or topics, he is a mild pessimist and can present the opposite view when Gregg is being too optimistic. They bickered about this during the survey but then came to an agreement about how it can still work for each partner. They felt that in some situations it was being unrealistic to think how great everything can be. That's when a pessimist will call themselves a realist!

In the survey, they had three answers that were not similar and may be considered a source of difficulty that they have managed to work through: they come from different socioeconomic backgrounds. However, because they communicate well and accept and respect each other's differences, over the twenty-one years together they have worked through the issues that come up from not having similar backgrounds—though it can still cause arguments.

When filling out the survey question "When the going gets tough you ..." Joe stated that he would rather walk away (from an argument), when he was not right. He felt it might avoid an argument. Gregg preferred to work through it.

When asked what was the secret for their success, Gregg answered, "knowing when to give in to an argument." He would rather be happy than right! Joe stated, "Enjoy each other's company and don't rely on your partner for happiness, find it within yourself. Opposites *can* attract."

They were very open. They came into the survey thinking they weren't a good match because they bicker often, but as the survey went on and I explained how differences can be beneficial, their mood changed. The bickering stopped, and they could see the value in each other's personality traits.

They scored a 90% on the survey and were happily surprised. They weren't sure they would score that high, because they felt they bickered too much. After we talked about the survey and discussed their differences and how that may have made them more compatible than they realized, their attitude changed. They were happy to realize how those differences had actually made them a good couple.

They were fun to interview, because I could see and understand what was going on and how easy it was to correct what they assumed was a flaw! By the end of our interview and conversation, they were very appreciative, and both appeared grateful for their partner!

***

Following are some of the remarks I got from doing phone interviews with couples who had been married over twenty years. I asked them what their secret was to longevity and having a good marriage. When they were done laughing at me for the "good marriage" remark, they had some more serious things to tell me. Here was their list:

1. Do whatever the wife says (this is the most common).
2. If your wife is happy, you will be happy (rather be happy than right).
3. Stay friends with open communication.
4. Use humor to defuse bad situations or disagreements.
5. Must respect each other.
6. Give them space to be who they are.

The first two may sound like a joke, but there is truth to what they say. Men who do not need to control their wives, but respect them enough to defer, can make much better husbands!

I truly believe if you do this work you will have a great start in your relationship. Thank you very much for letting my experiences help you in yours!